Creativity and Prayer

Creativity and Prayer

RUTH FOWKE
AND
PAM DODSON

eagle

Guildford, Surrey

Illustration Credits:
Front cover and Chapters 1, 3, 4, 7 and 8: Ruth Fowke
Chapters 2, 5, 6, 9 and 10: Pam Dodson.

British Library Cataloguing-in-Publication Data. A catalogue record for this book is available from the British Library.

Published in the UK by Eagle, an imprint of Inter Publishing Service (IPS) Ltd, St Nicholas House, 14 The Mount, Guildford, Surrey GU2 5HN.

Printed in Singapore

ISBN: 0 86347 278 8

Contents

Foreword

'Are you tired? Worn out? . . . Keep company with me and you'll learn to live freely and lightly.' That's how Eugene Peterson paraphrases Jesus' immortal invitation that many of us know off by heart: 'Come to me, all you who are weary and burdened . . . and I will give you rest' (Matthew 11:28).

If ever a generation needed to hear and heed that invitation it is our generation. Those of us who live in the stressed West can so easily be swept along in the currents of a culture that seems to insist that we live life at break-neck speed despite the inherent dangers of living life in the rapids. A friend recently spelled out just one of those dangers: 'I've only got one free day for the next month,' she confessed. 'The problem is that, when I'm so busy, the first thing that suffers is my prayer.'

Many readers of this book will identify with that sad confession. Many will therefore welcome and be grateful for the insights the authors pack into its pages. You don't have to be on your knees to pray, they insist. You can pray as you work, as you tend the garden, as you relax. For to pray simply means to keep in touch with God and we can tune into God's loving presence at any time and in any place.

How? In this joy-filled book, Ruth Fowke and Pam Dodson respond to that pertinent question.

They are well qualified to do so. They are both gifted, fulfilled women who enjoy life in all its fullness – women who bring glory to God by their zest for life, their aliveness and the emphasis they place on making and maintaining good, nurturing relationships. They are also both creative women. Watching them being re-energised by their God-given creativity was what prompted me to invite them to write this book in the first place. They not only foster their relationship with God as they work and as they walk, they turn their thoughts God-ward as they paint, as they immerse themselves in the wonder of creation or as they engage in activities like clay-modelling or journalling. Their enthusiasm for life is infectious.

Yet both know what it means to be still, to listen to God, to respond to God's love with every part of their being. As their book goes to print, I pray that it may inspire countless readers similarly to encounter God in a variety of ways and to become as contagiously alive as the authors are for, as one teacher of prayer claimed centuries ago: 'The glory of God is a man truly alive.' Or, as he might put it today: 'The glory of God is a man or a woman fully alive.'

Joyce Huggett
Derbyshire
June 1998

Preface

This book was conceived when we were on holiday together. We each then wrote our respective chapters and sent them to the other for comment. We are both greatly indebted to our friend, Margaret Old, formerly of Scripture Union, for kindly reading both manuscripts, and making invaluable comments. We hope her observations have prevented unnecessary repetition, especially in kindred subjects like nature and gardening.

We are also grateful to the various other friends who have shared their experiences with us, and allowed us to use some of them in these pages.

There are of course many forms of creativity we have not been able to include. Omissions had to be made for reasons of space, specialism, or because they are more adequately written about elsewhere. Notable exclusions are photography, all forms of needlecraft, bannermaking, basketry and working with wood.

We have restricted ourselves to those activities with which we are personally familiar, and hope that this will encourage readers to experiment with their own creative ways into prayer.

1

Enjoying Prayer

And God saw that it was good.
(Genesis 1:10,12,18,21,25,31)

One of the most enjoyable activities for me is to wander alone around the many small, interconnecting paths of the woodland area in the Royal Horticultural Gardens at Wisley. There I am without constraint of time, or of any specific goals. I just amble, observe and absorb. I am, as it were, mentally, emotionally and intellectually freewheeling; not trying to grasp, understand or achieve anything. Just being. Of course such precious times do not happen by themselves, I have to plan them into my diary. They are my equivalent of Adam and Eve walking with God in the refreshing cool of the evening, after their day's work was done. Just enjoying the world, and each other.

That for me is truly creative prayer. This chapter was in fact sketched out in those gardens as, notebook in hand, I wandered about. I was quietly alert to God in whatever form he might choose to communicate with me, but I was not trying to achieve anything. I was passively alert rather than actively striving at that time. Sometimes I stopped to pay closer attention to a plant, an insect or a bird, or to jot down a thought that sprang to mind, but most of the time I just freewheeled.

We need to regain the sense of enjoyment in prayer, as in the rest of life itself. Prayer both flows out of the life of the person, and into that life in one continuous, creative act. This is very like the process of breathing. We breathe in the air from outside our bodies, it mingles in our lungs as gases are exchanged and then we breathe out a part of our very selves. Prayer cannot be divorced from the lives we are leading. The more we enjoy life the more we can enjoy prayer. The more enjoyment we get in praying the more our lives are enriched.

Of course there are other aspects to prayer. There must always be reverence, but reverence and enjoyment are not in opposition to one another. There will be solemn times, especially times of sorrow and of penitence, but we must also learn to delight in God.

Throughout the Genesis account of creation we hear the refrain 'And God saw that it was good'. The last time it is used we read, 'and God saw all that he had made and it was very good'. Not just good, but very good. The acts of creation gave him pleasure.

There is in this account a sense of taking time over the formation of the cosmos. God took time off from the activity inherent in creation to review and to enjoy what he had done in each successive phase of the process. Also he seems to have paused in order to see each particular phase in the context of what was yet to come. Every phase was complete in itself, and yet at the same time none were fully completed until all were finished, and together they made a coherent whole.

In the following chapter of Genesis we read about 'trees that were pleasing to the eye and good for food'. Trees are not just utilitarian objects, providing fruit to eat, wood for fuel and building and leaves for a variety of uses according to species. They are also pleasing to the eye and that is a very important aspect of life which tends to be relegated to second place in our increasingly utilitarian world.

Western scientific rationalism has tended to overvalue left brain activity and consequently to allow right brain functions to wither through disuse, if not through downright disapproval of them. It is the left brain that does 'sensible' things like analysing, abstracting and doing things in sequence. It is most at home with words, numbers, precision diagrams and keeping good time. The right brain deals more with synthesis than with analysis, putting things together, seeing relationships and how one thing influences another. It likes to deal spatially rather than sequentially, and uses metaphors more than facts.

This is the 'eureka' part of the brain, freewheeling and juggling, letting thoughts come and go until suddenly ideas fall into place with astonishing clarity. It does not reason as left brain activity does, it cannot be controlled and it does not make judgements. When right brain activity is in the ascendancy there is a sense of timelessness and of creative reverie.

In this book we are writing mainly about what have come to be called right brain activities, although of course the left brain has to be involved as well. In practice, we dodge between the two types of process all the time. They are complementary ways of seeing and responding to the world in which we live and we need to engage both in prayer, as in all of life.

The types of prayer with which many of us are most familiar engage the left side of the brain more often than they utilise the right side. We are brought up to equate prayer with using words. Sometimes we use so many in intercession, confession, thanksgiving and supplication that we are almost in danger of trying to tell God what to do! This book aims to redress the balance and to encourage the reader to experiment in ways of being less verbal and cerebral when we relate to the divine presence. Many of us need to let go of the utilitarian outlook that tells us prayer must be meaningful, in some way productive of something tangible and useful.

Most of us need to spend considerably more time 'wasting time' with God, just being in his presence, delighting in him, paying attention to him in a freewheeling sort of way. Without realising it we tend to take into prayer times the secular striving for every second to be clearly productive and useful. We unconsciously expect to 'get somewhere' in prayer, to 'get something' out of it; some increase in understanding, some new insight, something definable that we can hang onto, rather than being content with the relationship for its own intrinsic sake.

As well as the enjoyment so evident in the creation narrative I also suspect there is an element of playfulness, almost of 'let's try it and see what happens'. There is such lavish diversity in each category mentioned, 'every living and moving thing with which the water teems, according to their kinds, and every winged bird according to its kind.' The waters as well as the earth just teem with myriads of diverse creatures, simply because they, and the making of them, please God. Some creatures may appear uninteresting to us, generally when they show little movement, have few interactions or are of drab colouring, while others are distinctly humorous in their movement, or their colour or in some other characteristic. Some are ephemeral, with an incredibly short lifespan, others have the potential for really long lives. And God saw that all of them, individually as well as in broad categories, are good. The sheer wanton, enjoyable abundance of it all. God was at work, and at times he was also playing.

Contemplating creation certainly brings us into contact with the diversity, the immensity and the imagination of the Creator. The God who dreamt up such a wealth of contrasting creatures – the ant and the giraffe, the wallaby and the warthog, the ladybird and the lion – is surely pleased when we too dare to be creative. We need at times to get beyond the solemnity and awesomeness of God and to approach him with a reverent lightness of spirit.

Often we need to loosen up and allow the bubbling up of sheer fun that culminates in laughter at the goodness, and the absurdity, of life and of the Giver of life.

To play is to originate or to participate in spontaneous activity that is undertaken for its own sake, simply for its own intrinsic sake. There is no ulterior motive and nothing in particular has to be achieved. There is no other goal than the play itself. Clearly this requires inner freedom, freedom to experiment without prejudging the outcome. To enter into play we must for a while suspend logical thought and all critical judgement. We just try things out, and see if they fit the moment. We experiment and invent anew for ourselves ways to begin to make sense of experiences and thoughts we cannot quite articulate.

In play we are simply involved with what we are doing. Just watch small children, their complete dedication to the task of the moment. For a brief while they are outside time, nothing else at all impinges on them. Their whole being is concentrated on this one present activity. It is play, and it is serious. It is serious, life-enhancing stuff, and it is also play. Jesus said that 'unless you change and become like little children, you will never enter the kingdom of heaven' (Matt 18:3) and I am sure that their uncomplicated, uncritical immediacy is at least one of the attributes we are to encourage in ourselves.

When there is no room for play in our lives we cease to grow. When we cease to grow we begin to atrophy, spiritually as well as physically. Margaret Guenther in her book *Toward Holy Ground* speaks of watching calves in the field[1]:

> they run with abandon and without apparent purpose, wheel about in sharp turns, are joined by their fellows in a glorious romp, and then stop as suddenly as they started. Then I look at their mothers – great, stolid beasts – and wonder what has happened . . . When did the joy of cool air and soft turf and blue sky cease to exhilarate? When did it stop being fun to run as fast as they could, just for the fun of it?

And she concludes, 'We dare not let ourselves become ponderous, too heavy to move. Play exists for its own sake.'

We need to actively delight in the child who exists somewhere inside each of us. For some this might mean learning first to tolerate their inner child, so that in time they may come to welcome and enjoy the richness that the child within them can give to their lives in general, and to prayer in particular. Being in touch with our inner child can help us to

17

be more playful, more real, more truly ourselves in the presence of God. Playing helps us to be more relaxed, more genuinely prayerful. When we pray with a playful attitude, or play in prayerful mode (it's much the same thing), we are not asking for anything, not expecting to get anything from this time, other than the enjoyment of God in this present moment. We are not expecting to achieve anything, not setting out to gain any special insight or knowledge, we are just spending time, investing time, in developing a relationship with God.

Unfortunately our productivity-oriented culture has conditioned us to consider that time spent without any special purpose must be wasted time. Unless we are aware of deriving some benefit from an activity, unless our prayer time itself results in some definite thought or feeling, we are likely to regard the time as misused. If we have not advanced in some specific way, then our culture, often including sections of Christian culture, assumes that we have squandered the time.

In one respect, playing is pure carelessness. When we play, we concentrate on the play, and for a time we let go of the usual cares of life. Having times of genuine care-lessness is an aid to spiritual, mental, emotional and physical health. The AV rendering of Philippians 4:6 is 'Be careful for nothing', which the NIV has as, 'Do not be anxious about anything'. In our anxiety-ridden age we need ways and means and times to step aside from the cares and worries that so often engross us.

Most of us need to take time out from the things that usually preoccupy us, however legitimate and pressing they are. We need to take time to wind down. It takes a conscious effort to cease from doing all those things that quite properly occupy the bulk of our time. Most people find it hard to 'just be'. We are brainwashed into having to be demonstrably productive, into being able to show our achievements, with the result that many feel guilty if they are not busy and active all the time, including the time they spend in prayer. Our very busyness has unwittingly made us less than human. We DO so much, and lose ourselves in the process. We need to relinquish our addiction to resembling human dynamos and learn again how to be human beings rather than human doings.

This applies even more to what goes on inside our heads than it does to whatever our bodies might do. So often our minds go babbling on long after our tongue is silent. It is hard to attain inner stillness, to quieten the constant activity of our minds. We intend to pray, we aim to open ourselves very deliberately and wholeheartedly to God, but soon find that our minds drift back to yet more planning, reasoning, arguing and analysing. There is almost ceaseless chatter going on in our minds.

Sometimes we are so action-oriented that we tend to relate most to the God of action, to the God-who-DOES-things. When we fall into this trap we are likely to lose sight of the God who IS, the one who calls himself simply I AM. In this state we are more aware of the God of power than we are of the God of presence. At such times a very good prelude to prayer, and sometimes forming the prayer itself, is to stop the headlong rush of life for a while, to lighten up on the seriousness of it all, and to just freewheel. That surely is one aspect of playing. Just being at home as part of God's creation. Doodling with life. Dawdling with the King. Just being.

Once when I was running a workshop on prayer I decided to attempt an ABC of the subject and I wanted to include humour. The letter H had already been used for honesty so I had to use J for joking instead. That seemed to the course members to be going too far and we had a lively discussion on the subject. The prevailing opinion seemed to be that one just does not joke with God. Well, certainly not in the way that is really veiled malice, or the rather barbed usage that often underlies the defensive retort, 'I was only joking'. I am not advocating the laughter of derision, but I do firmly believe there is a place for the laughter of enjoyment that just bubbles up from within. There is no place for the hollow mirth that turns people into an unhappy laughing stock, but there is a large place for laughing at the sheer pleasure of living.

Almost everyone responds with delight to the spontaneous chuckle of young children. There is something deeply satisfying and infectious about the unselfconscious chortle that erupts when they are pleased. As Sydney Harris so rightly points out,

'God cannot be solemn, or he would not have blessed man with the incalculable gift of laughter'. And even Martin Luther is on record as saying 'If you're not allowed to laugh in Heaven, I don't want to go there'. To joke, to say or do something merely for the fun of it because we see and delight in the many contrasts of life, and in what seems to us at the time to be absurd, is to appreciate the fullness and the richness of creation. When did you last laugh during, or in, prayer?

Be Creative

1. Make a list of the things you most enjoy doing, the things that make you feel most alive, most free, most truly yourself.

   Note whether they are active, productive, focused activities of 'doing', or the more unfocused times when you flow with what comes, the product of 'just being'.

   Do you have a reasonable balance between the two, or is there a bias towards one more than the other?

   Use your list to reflect on, and pray about, the balance (or otherwise) in this stage of your life.

2. Play in the presence of God; just delight in his presence and in his playfulness. Here is a suggestion to get you going but anything, just anything, will do.

   Crumple a piece of paper into a ball. Toss it in

the air, throw it at the window, roll it along the ground. Notice your thoughts and feelings as you do this, they are part of your present awareness.

Ask yourself how God might be regarding you at this moment.

Let these things be the focus of your prayer today.

3. Prayer Alphabet
   Reflect on the following list, and add to it as you go.
   Tick those that you agree with.
   Make another mark against those that are part of your current prayer life.
   Consider those words that do not seem to you to be valid prayer. Discuss the matter with the Lord.

   Adoration. Anger.
   Breath. Body Posture.
   Confession.
   Discovery. Delighting in . . . Desert.
   Envisioning. Examining.
   Friendship.
   Grieving. Growing.
   Honesty.
   Intercession. Imagination.
   Joking. Joy. Journalling.
   Knowing.
   Letting go. Laptime. Language.

Meditation.

Non-verbal. New patterns.

Opening oneself. Obedience.

Praying in the promises of God. Persistence. Petition.

Questioning.

Receiving. Reverence. Relationship.

Struggling. Structured, and unstructured.

Tuning in. Trinity. Tension.

Unceasing.

Vulnerable. Variety. Visualising answers. Verbalising.

Waiting. Walking. Warfare.

X – THE UNKNOWN. We cannot control God.

Yelling.

Zealous.

2

Praying with Nature

*'Consider the ravens . . . consider how
the lilies grow.'
(Luke 12:24,27)*

When God created the world, he was pleased with
all that he had created. Sometimes I try to imagine
that original garden, with its trees, flowers of every
kind, the river running through, and perhaps a
waterfall and lake. Everything would be flourishing, the ecology working perfectly and there would
be all that mankind could need. When God made
the animals and all the other creatures, he made
the man and woman responsible for their welfare.
Whether you believe in every word literally or not,
it is clear that God was and is the source of all life.
He loves the whole of His creation, and goes on loving it. The more we love it, cherish it and learn
from it, the more we are in harmony with the
Creator.

Jesus loved to be in the open air, to walk in the
fields, sit on the hillside and walk by (and on!) the
sea. So much of his teaching took illustrations from
nature and more often than not his parables spoke
of natural things his hearers could see around

them. In fact, nearly all his teaching was in parables. No wonder that when we have our eyes open and our hearts in tune with God, we also see parables all around us.

When not consciously learning lessons, we can celebrate the wonder of God's creation and feel our hearts stirred in praise and worship. Looking out of the window and seeing the white foam on the waves, the gulls circling overhead riding on the currents of air, makes my spirit soar with them. Seeing the trees bending in the wind and the sky constantly changing shape and colour, I marvel at the forces of nature that march on in spite of all that mankind tries to do to them. In the garden I glory in the numerous shapes and colours of the flowers, each bloom a miracle of intricacy. Watching the tiny insects, busy about their work, or feeling the bark of trees, I am surprised at the different textures and designs. Walking down by the cliffs my dog tears up and down with exuberant joy, giving such a good example of enjoying the moment, and being aware of every sight, sound and smell. We do need to take time to enjoy God's creation. Living in a busy, hurrying world, we must make time to wonder and know that God is God, in order to function better.

Annabel Robinson has written:

> God has created an amazingly complex world for us to enjoy, and the more we know about it the more we are able to appreciate its Maker. I love the insight given to us about Solomon in 1 Kings 4:33 where 'he described plant life, from the cedar of Lebanon to the hyssop that grows out of walls. He also taught about animals and birds, reptiles and fish.' His wisdom came from observation and study of the world around him.[1]

One early morning I went into the garden and picked a single red rose. It was a bud that was beginning to open, and the dew was still on it. The beauty of it stirred my heart and made me want to praise its Creator. I placed it in a single bloom vase and stood it on my prayer desk. Just the action of doing that seemed like an act of worship. The drops of dew glistening on the petals reminded me that 'new every morning is his love'. Marvelling at the graceful curves of the petals, protecting the centre, as yet unseen, I thanked God that there is always mystery about him. There is always more for us to discover, and some things we will never know till we see him face to face. Enjoying the warmth of colour, the bright red fading to deep orange at the base of the petals, made me feel wrapped around in the love of God. I smelled the delicate fragrance and remembered that 'God . . . through us spreads everywhere the fragrance of the knowledge of him. For we are to God the aroma of Christ' (2 Cor 2:14,15). That seems almost incredible, but I prayed that in some way, today, that would be true of me. Knowing that during the course of the day, the bud would open and reveal its centre, my prayer was that I would be open to all that God would say to me and do with me.

A few days later, sitting at my prayer desk, I noticed that my beautiful rose was drooping and dying, and the greenery had become dry and brittle. Although the vase had been filled up the day before, the heat had used up all the moisture. I felt mean that I had not supplied enough water to keep it fresh. This made me think of how I dry up and lose spiritual vitality if not adequately resourced by the Living Water. Usually it is my fault, as Jesus is always saying, 'If anyone is thirsty, let him come to me and drink'. But I can also remember times, especially when working in Nepal, when from sheer hard work and lack of Christian fellow-ship I had dried up. How we need to take time to stop and stare, and just be with the Lord.

'Praying with nature' is one way to do that. So that day my dried up flower prompted me to pray a prayer written by Julian of Norwich:

Holy Spirit, Spirit of love, Spirit of discipline.
    In the silence
Come to us and bring us your peace;
Rest in us that we may be tranquil and still;
Speak to us as each heart needs to hear;
Reveal to us things hidden and things longed
    for;
Rejoice in us that we may praise and be glad;
Pray in us that we may be at one with you
    and with each other;
Refresh and renew us from your Living Springs
    of water.
Holy Spirit, dwell in us that your light may
    shine through us,
And that in our hearts you may find your
    homeliest home
    and endless dwelling.

                                    Amen

Out in the street, a park or the countryside, we can imagine that God is walking with us and opening our eyes, as if to see for the very first time. As we delight in all we see and hear, imagine how much greater our joy would be if we had made it. We are part of what he has made. Brother Ramon says 'How absolutely central is the truth that we are first of all part of nature, though we are a very special part, that which is conscious of God. In solitude, one is surrounded by beings which perfectly obey God. This leaves only one place open for me, and if I occupy that place then I too am fulfilling his will . . . One has to be alone, under the sky, before everything falls into place and one finds one's own place in the midst of it all.'[2]

We don't need to be in the countryside or by the sea to enjoy and pray with nature. Skies can be seen even in a crowded town. The rising and setting sun often creates amazing colours and shapes, and speaks of the glory of God. It may remind us that, 'The sun of righteousness will rise with healing in its wings'(Mal 4:2), and lead us to pray about areas of healing that we or others need. As the sun goes down, we may remember people in more distant lands, for whom the day is just starting. Stormy skies will remind us of the cosmic battle that is constantly being waged between the forces of good and evil. The sky at night is often awesome, and the stars and the moon remind us of the immensity of the universe and of our own smallness. Our great God not only created all this, but is aware even of the sparrow that falls to the ground. It somehow puts our own troubles into perspective. Wherever we are, in town or country, we can be conscious of the elements and allow them to stimulate our prayer.

The wind reminds us of the Holy Spirit, and we pray for his working in our hearts and in our nation. The rain, too, symbolises the coming of God's blessing and refreshing, and we make an act of receiving that blessing from the Lord and praying for others. We don't even have to go outside to pray with nature. A bowl of fruit, some vegetables or a pot plant, may be perceived as a parable and turned into prayer. Some cress or herbs can be grown on a window-sill, wondered at as it springs up, and in due course tasted with relish and thankfulness.

It is helpful sometimes to 'Pray with the Seasons'. Each one has a great deal to teach us about God and about ourselves, which will draw us into worship and prayer. In autumn we glory in the brilliant colours, the gold reminding us of the Kingship of Christ. Then the leaves dry up and drop. It is a season, not only of 'mellow fruitfulness' but also of surrender. It is a letting go of the flamboyance of summer, a stripping in preparation for the harsh weather. The trees conserve their energy and moisture. There are times when we may feel we are being stripped of past fruitful activity, and we feel sad. Then, if we can become aware that we are conserving energy for the next phase, it gives us a more positive view of the future. I was feeling rather like that when, a few years ago, I was facing retirement from medical work and moving away. While at a retreat I wrote this very amateurish poem which nevertheless expressed my feelings at the time:

Is This Autumn?

Is this Autumn, Lord, for me?
The leaves are falling, one by one.
Important things that make up life,
That give it shape and certainty.

Summer time has been so good,
So much to do and play and pray,
With growing things all flourishing,
Pressing along to reach today.

Will it be empty, Lord, for me?
No patients to treat, no committee to chair?
Will relationships cease to be?
Will the changes be hard to bear?

'Not so my child,' He says to me,
'Another Spring is on the way,
'The Winter comes to rest the earth,
'And then new things will come to birth.'

Then winter comes with its cold and darkness. It can be depressing, but it has its own beauty. Frost makes intricate patterns on the windows, and silvers the spiders' webs, and snow bending the boughs of trees or on the rooftops evokes worship. Winter does seem to be frozen and sterile, so it is easy to forget that underneath the soil much is going on. The roots are growing deep and strong, ready for the reawakening of spring. The earth is

resting and quiet, and the animals are hibernating. Someone has said that 'Hope is the winter name of God'. How apt were the words of Jesus in John 12:24, 'Unless a kernel of wheat falls to the ground and dies, it remains only a single seed. But if it dies, it produces many seeds.' The earth appears to die, but in reality it is only sleeping, cherishing the seed until the time of reawakening.

All this has an echo in our own souls. We all have times of darkness, when we feel frozen and unproductive. It is part of being human. Even the greatest saints have had such times, when even God seems far away. Just as winter is necessary to prepare for further growth, so it is with us; we need the resting times to build up our resources for the next stage of the journey. The paralysis of nature in winter has been seen as the northern equivalent of the biblical desert, when there seems to be no life. The difference is that winter passes and a new spring wakes up. God seems to allow these bleak times to strengthen our roots. Maria Boulding says, 'Looking back, you know that these times brought you closer to the Lord of the Winter, that it was necessary for you to go through them. In the Winters of your prayer, when there seems to be nothing but darkness and a general frozenness, hold on, wait for God, He will come.' Here is a prayer for the wintry times expressed by Brother Ramon:

When the winter of my life
Threatens me with pain and death,
Leave me not in loneliness
To its cold and icy breath;
Breathe upon me from above
And enfold me in your love.[3]

It is winter as I am writing this. When I woke up this morning, there was a delicate white tracery on the windows and a thick layer of snow covering everything, quite an unusual thing here by the sea. Although it was long before dawn, there was an ethereal glow over the whole scene. When, a little later, I took the dog for a walk, I almost felt guilty, as our footsteps marked the unsullied snow. I need not have worried. By the time we came back, they were covered by a fresh fall of snow. It reminded me of the words in Psalm 32:1: 'Blessed is he whose transgressions are forgiven, whose sins are covered.' I prayed that I might have a pure heart, to see God in everything, not only in nature, but also in everything that happens to me.

When spring comes, there is a general sense of relief. The sap rises in the trees and shrubs, the leaves begin to appear and new shoots poke through the hard ground. The whole earth begins to vibrate with a sense of expectation and anticipation. As the frosts pass, the spring bulbs begin to bloom, and God's vitality enlivens us all. There is an air of excitement around, and we can pray that the Lord will do a new thing in us. It is so easy to become complacent and self-satisfied, when God wants us to grow and develop, bringing glory to his name.

This poem-prayer of Ulrich Schaffer's speaks of this:

I sense your drive
To flow through me
Into the smallest blood vessels
Because you want to be my heartblood
In all the passages of my life
And you want to become visible in the leaves
And the fruit that I bear.

Spread out in me
Press forward penetrate pierce and flow
Even if at times
I want to repeal this invitation

Being afraid of your ways with me.

Circulate in me
Change and renew
Because I know
That only your Spirit
Can bring real life and fruit.[4]

Although spring is an exciting and revitalising time, it is not all sweetness and light. The sheer eruption of life is so strong, it may cause disruption as it pushes aside the things in its path. This speaks to us of the 'violence of unconditional love', concentrating on the one thing necessary, which is growth. God's love will go to all lengths to stimulate us to grow. Pruning, too, is something all gardeners know about and recognise as being necessary for growth: 'He cuts off every branch in me that bears no fruit, while every branch that does bear fruit he prunes so that it will be even more fruitful' (John 15:2).

As spring gradually merges into summer, nature blossoms in every way. All its abundance is demonstated in a profusion of colours and fragrances. It is as if the whole of creation is singing a psalm of praise and is lost for words in its joy. While blooming, the flowers are also making seeds, and the potential is enormous. One day I went into the garden and picked some sweet peas. They were a mixture of mauves, purples and whites. I added some white marguerites and a few purple spikes. I arranged them, with some greenery, in a glass vase, and put them in front of me as I settled down to prayer. The colours reminded me of the majesty and purity of God and led me into worship. In fact, the actual picking and arranging of them, to me, was an act of worship. Then I noticed that one of the sweet peas already had a seed pod on it, a promise of future rebirth and fruitfulness.

The way plants flourish depends so much on the type of soil in which they are planted, and the enviromental conditions. In fact this applies to all animal life as well, and is true of us too. Under some conditions we flourish, in others we become weak and stunted. Think for a moment, what things help you to blossom as a personality and as a Christian? We are unable to choose the environment into which we are born, but we are making choices every day about the content of our lives. One thing we all need is a sense of being loved and accepted, and we can be sure that our Heavenly Father does that for all of us. He loves us with an everlasting love. He says we are 'precious in his eyes'. He made us and he loves what he made. In fact he rejoices over us. No matter how many mistakes we believe we have made, he goes on loving. He nurtures and feeds us like a good and skilful gardener. He does this, not just for our own sake, but so that others will see his beauty and be blessed by him. We can pray like the writer of the Song of Solomon, 'Come, south wind! Blow on my garden, that its fragrance may spread abroad' (4:16).

Suggestions for Prayer Activity

1. Take a walk with God through a garden, city street, canal bank, park or countryside. Become aware of the season – its colour, shape and texture. Collect a few things appropriate to this season; flowers, berries, seed pods, leaves or twigs and make an arrangement when you get back. Allow the Holy Spirit to lead you to the things which are significant for you. Keep your collection for some time and let it lead you into prayer.

2. Fill a tray or a box lid with some sand or soil. Make a miniature oasis with stones, bark, small plants, grass, moss etc. and add a small container of water to represent the things you know are essential to your spiritual life. Are you being adequately resourced? Pray about this.

3. Make a collection or arrangement, which represents a situation about which you are concerned and are praying about. It may include such things as a letter, a candle, a flower, a map or a tool. This can become a reminder for intercession.

4. Pick a stone, or pebble, either polished or rough, that seems to draw you in some way. Each one has its unique characteristics and colours. Study it carefully. Caress it, love it. Is there something about it that reminds you of yourself? Be aware

that God made it and loves it. Allow God to speak to you through it, and then offer it to him, perhaps putting it by a candle to represent Christ.

> Take my life and let it be
> Consecrated, Lord to thee;
> Take my moments and my days,
> Let them flow in ceaseless praise.

If you would like to experience more of Praying with Nature in a very beautiful place, I suggest you write to Ann Persson, Highmoor Hall, Highmoor, Henley-on-Thames, Oxfordshire RG9 5DH, for their 'Time for Reflection' brochure.

3

Creating a Home

The place where you are . . . is holy.
(Exodus 3:5)

'Come to an Owl Hunt', said the invitation. It was nothing for conservationists to get worried about, only a single person's way of getting friends to mix and talk together. Some did not know each other at all and they enjoyed wandering about the garden, chatting as they looked for hidden owls made of various materials. The hostess had discovered that some activity like this got the evening off to a better start than strangers making polite but perhaps rather stilted conversation to each other. It also freed her to greet guests as they arrived. The larger collection from which those owls were chosen had previously been useful when entertaining a family one wet weekend. The children had loved exploring the house, counting the owls dotted about and reaching a different total every time.

Today, an increasing number of adults live alone, and some find the multiple demands of single life rather daunting. On the plus side they do have more flexibility regarding how they use their homes, and how they choose to do so will be a mix-

Holy Ground,

Ruth F

40

ture of personality, opportunity, imagination, effort and enjoyment. The concepts behind the ideas in this chapter are equally applicable for those who live alone, in a family group or as unrelated adults sharing a house.

Home is where we belong, it is our space and our place whether for a week, a year or as long as we can foresee. It is where we can just 'be', and also where we can express ourselves in our surroundings, be they a temporary bed-sit, a rented flat or our own house. It is a place of rest from work, but also requires work to keep it going. It is a place of relaxation and of enjoyment in making it interesting, colourful, beautiful and welcoming; where we can thrive rather than passively survive.

One home I know is full of intriguing things found out and about in the countryside over the years: old tools, discarded pottery, unusual bits of wood, odd-shaped stones and deserted birds nests. There is even one nest made entirely of bits of soft wire, the answer to the puzzlement of the owner of the hedge where it was found. He had been wondering why he was always having to replace the rings used to tie up his climbing plants. On showing me these assorted treasures my friend kept saying, 'Isn't nature wonderful, isn't God great?'

The actions of creating and maintaining a home become prayer as we deliberately invite Christ to make it his home too. Remembering that this home of mine is also his, offering it as a Bethany for him again, is surely to 'sit at his feet' even as we hurry about our daily tasks. People of many religions, Jewish, Hindu and others, show their faith in their homes. Christianity has its roots in Judaism where all that was put into a home, all that was said and done there, were expressions of faith. We too need to delight in our faith, expressing it openly in our homes, and in the way we live out our lives there.

I am frequently encouraged by that lovely account of the two sisters whose home was always open to Jesus. It was the place where he rested on his way back to Jerusalem for the last time. He knew that he had to fulfil his destiny and complete this journey despite his awareness that he would face betrayal, rejection and a cruel death. He set his face resolutely to go through with all that lay ahead, and he desperately needed this quiet haven of acceptance along the way. Mary understood his need, and stayed with him as he talked to her brother Lazarus, but their sister Martha was flustered by all the practical things that had to be done. It was not just the getting of a meal for one extra, but she probably tried to make it a special one for their honoured guest. She, like us, was distracted by all the preparations that precede producing any meal. On this occasion Jesus said that Mary had understood his most pressing need, and was staying with him instead of rushing around getting ready for him.

Somehow we have to learn to have a Mary heart whilst engaging in all the necessary Martha activities. It is possible to combine the attitude of both those sisters as we work in and around our homes. Instead of having the radio or TV on as we go about routine chores, the doing of them may be a good time to listen to an instructional or devotional tape, or to sing along with a worshipful recording. Or we may choose to restock the larder of our minds by memorising Bible verses, and reflecting on their relevance to our current situation. Each of us needs to find ways of transforming the many routine tasks associated with running any home and turn them into an integral part of our prayer pattern.

Every single action during each ordinary day is an opportunity for a one-sentence prayer, born out of the thoughts and feelings associated with the tasks being undertaken. Window cleaning is one of the many jobs that I habitually put off. After weeks of seeing beautiful sunsets through a hazy smear, I finally got around to tackling the job one brisk autumn morning. It was one of those days that invigorate, I was rejoicing in the sunshine and in the surge of energy that I was experiencing. Praise for both welled up within me and as I rubbed at stubborn marks left by unwary insects, it was natural to ask the Lord what stained areas there were in me that needed his attention, and mine. An otherwise boring chore became a conversational time between us.

We need to recapture and rekindle the spirituality of the ancient Celts. They had a prayer for every common activity throughout the day and the year, like putting on clothes, lighting a fire (no central heating in those days) and turning the first sod of earth. They would breathe a prayer with everything they did, right through from awakening in the morning to settling down for sleep at night, without any distinction between the sacred and the secular.

Members of one church I know take turns to make the Communion bread required for the month ahead. They are encouraged to do this in a reflective attitude, and are given guidelines for praying through each stage of the process. They may be able to choose the day and time of their breadmaking, but I wonder how many of us are able to get anywhere near the assertion of Brother Lawrence. Working full-time in the kitchen of his monastery he called himself 'the lord of all pots and pans' and commented that:

> The time of business does not with me differ from the time of prayer; and in the noise and clatter of my kitchen, while several persons are at the same time calling for different things, I possess God in as great tranquillity as if I were upon my knees at the blessed sacrament.

Of course we will not always do chores in a heavenward frame of mind, but it is a useful attitude to cultivate. I like Richard Foster's practical approach in his book simply entitled *Prayer*. He says:

> But what about those times that feel decidedly

unspiritual – when we have a confrontation with the children or a disagreement with our spouse . . . Frankly, beyond the desperation prayers . . . ('O God, help!'), I have found that I cannot pray during these times. So rather than trying to fool myself by piously pretending constant communion, what I do in such situations is to ask God for a time out . . . The question is not whether we fail again and again – that is a given; the question is whether over, a period of time we are developing a practised habit of divine fellowship.[1]

Central to all that goes on in every home are probably the meals served there. The preparation and eating of meals is often the core, the pivotal activity, the very heart of a home, especially when they are taken with others. When they are to be eaten alone it is a great opportunity for communion with God, offering an intimate and personal time to be deliberately shared with him. When all the stages are considered, the planning, shopping, preparation and clearing away afterwards, this one essential function probably uses up more time, energy and thought than any other domestic activity. Cooking itself is a great opportunity for creative expression, for paying attention to combinations of colour, texture, taste and seasonings. This applies whether you are following a recipe or making it up as you go along, and there is further scope for creativity in the venue, presentation and serving of the meal.

Writing in the first issue of *Day by Day with God* (daily Bible readings by women, for women), Alice Stibbe tells of how she often felt guilty at her inability to continue her BC (before children) times of prayer. Like so many mothers of young children she found it was just not possible to keep to scheduled times as their needs always seemed to upset any agenda. Then she discovered that the simple, deliberate act of taking off her shoes as she stood at the kitchen sink reminded her that she was on holy ground and in God's presence, even (perhaps especially?) while doing the chores. It is that sense of companionship with God that can become prayer as we tidy up, yet again, after whatever activity has been going on in the home.

In our excessively activist culture, meals are no longer as important as they once were. All too often they have become hurried affairs, frequently being regarded as necessary but unfortunate interruptions to the true business, and inevitable business, of life. Fast food, snacks at the desk or in the car, ready-made meals, microwave ovens and dinners in front of the TV have become commonplace. They may be necessary or expedient much of the time, but increasingly people are rediscovering the importance of eating as an enjoyable and necessary social activity. With everyone pursuing different activities, some families, and those in shared households, have to work hard to establish a regular corporate meal at sometime during the week.

How it is used and when it is held will obviously depend on the particular ages and interests of the various members, but it does establish the principle of spending time together and talking with one another. Those who live alone have to make an even greater effort in this regard. They have to plan ahead and invite guests who are compatible with each other, so that it will be an interesting and stimulating time for all.

Meals are also a golden opportunity, and sometimes the only occasion that some will realistically get, for praying with others. Some households like to sing a thanksgiving together, while in others different members take it in turns to compose or read a grace on behalf of all. Some couples, and even whole families, do still value a longer time of shared devotions together. The renowned leprosy surgeon Paul Brand, writing the Foreword to Eddie Askew's book *Cross Purposes* says:

> Breakfast in our home is never the same without a closing meditation and prayer from one of your lovely devotional books. It's a mistake to read more than one chapter at a time. Each needs to be savoured, with lingering appreciation, making each prayer one's own, even while we savour our last sips of coffee.[2]

Of course the advisability, as well as the opportunity, of any household praying together, whether at meals or at any other time, will change over the years as the ages and composition of its members alters. It is generally easier to do so when children are small, or after they have grown up and gone their own ways, than in their teenage years. People who regularly eat alone, and seldom pray with anyone else, are missing out on two creative fellowship occasions. Sometimes it is hard to find the space and the privacy to pray, even supposing one can carve out and safeguard the time. Few households now have the luxury of a whole room to set apart for prayer. Some find it possible to designate a particular area where it is understood that anyone using it wants and expects to be left undisturbed. This may only be a corner of the least used room, or even a cleared out cupboard, but place as well as time has to be found. I heard of one young woman in a temporarily crowded household who found her answer was to sit on the stairs to read.

The need to be alone at times with private thoughts does have to be explicitly recognised and honoured, although this is easier in some cultures than in others. In the Tagalog language of the Philippines the word for 'alone' is apparently the same as for 'sad', and if you do sit alone someone is very likely to come up and join you out of concern and politeness. In northern Canada the Inuit people have found their own unique solution. With only the one communal living and sleeping area, and freezing temperatures outside, they have adopted the convention that anyone who turns their face to the wall is regarded as simply 'not there'. They are totally ignored until they choose to turn around and face into the room once again.

However and whenever we manage to achieve it, a creative Christian home does need to provide the opportunity and the atmosphere that encourages and facilitates both private and corporate prayer. Those who live alone may have the privilege of offering their sunny patio, a secluded corner of the garden, or the spare room as a refuge for friends who do not have tranquillity or privacy in their own homes. These attributes are as necessary for some creative activities as they are for times more specifically set apart for prayer, and even more needed when the two activities are to be combined. Some people with suitable houses are happy to put a room at the disposal of anyone in need of quiet and privacy. The Diocese of Guildford, and probably others too, has a register of such houses.

As well as having opportunities for times of withdrawing from others in a noisy, crowded, busy world, people also need to celebrate, laugh and have fun together. The birthday parties of childhood tend to give way to special family excursions, then to outings with peers only, and eventually to other ways of marking milestones. The form and timing of any festivity will depend on the occasion being celebrated, and on the preferences of the participants. Some like predictability and tend to evolve their own traditions, which then become a valued part of any celebration. Others revel in the unusual and the unexpected, so for them an element of surprise is likely to be a necessary part of any good festivity.

A problem may arise when an individual with a preference for one way of celebrating is the odd one out in their particular family or group. As long as this is recognised as a genuine difference of temperament and not the individual being difficult or the group uncaring, it is usually possible to find a satisfying way of observing the occasion together. Give and take on all sides, laced with understanding, will find a fun way through the personality minefield.

People who live alone often have to plan and provide their own celebrations, according to their interests and circumstances. Some hire a hall for very special occasions, others prefer to share the event with fewer, more intimate friends. One chose to mark a winter birthday in her own home with just two friends for company. They all enjoyed painting, and spent the time companionably in each other's company, using different media and breaking off to relish a meal together, spending a quiet but deeply satisfying day.

Someone else I know has creative days in her home, when friends come to experiment with clay and a variety of paints, or making a collage either alone or with others. Sometimes this is specifically in the context of prayer, and always there is the informal opportunity to share discoveries and insights with each other. Occasionally another friend has held a play evening, with a number of board and card games available, giving variety and hilarity when half the people from each table move on to another. There are so many ways of using a home to create companionship, to the glory of God.

Some anniversaries and other memorable occasions belong exclusively to a particular family, but others are shared ones. Today there is a great deal of commercial exploitation of events like Mother's Day and Father's Day. Even the great Christian festivals of Christmas and Easter are in danger of being taken over by mammon, but they can be reclaimed and again become the focus of true celebration. Make the lighting of an Advent candle something of an occasion, a reverent opportunity to savour with anticipation the birth of the Saviour. If a crib scene is a prominent part of the decorations it will become more meaningful when the baby is absent from the manger until Christmas Eve, and the wise men only added following a further interval. This is after all a time to 'ponder all these things in the heart' as Mary herself did, and to provide a welcome interlude amongst busy preparations.

One year I visited friends who always do an especially festive Easter breakfast. The table was vibrant with colour; cheerful yellow candles in bright spring-green holders, napkins and crockery continuing the colour scheme, and the celebratory food was served with such joy that we lived the resurrection, as well as talked about it.

Be Creative

1 Make a list of the tasks that you do frequently. Each week write a prayer about one of them, or copy one, and so compile your own prayer book.

2. When you find yourself becoming most Martha-ish . . . pause. Recall the presence of God, the three persons of the Trinity, right there with you fully understanding the things that are pressurising you.

   Take some deep breaths and look at the sky; just look. It will help you to refocus, and will allow your right brain a chance to be heard. Let the sky be an open window through which you and God can meet and dialogue about your concerns. Continue that dialogue as you return to your work.

3. Light a candle and place it where you can see it as you eat. Let it remind you of Christ who is the Light of the World, and also of your own life.

4. If you live with others, find three ways, and a place, in which you can enjoy more personal space. Also find three ways that you can give similar opportunities to the others in your home.

   If you live alone find three ways and times of celebrating something with others.

4

In the Garden

Pray . . . on all occasions.
(Ephesians 6:18)

References to seeds and plants, trees and fruit abound in Scripture, encouraging us to reflect on them as we move about looking after our own plants. There is also that lovely statement by the Son of God that 'I am the true vine and my Father is the gardener' (John 15:1). No wonder that we want to garden under such a Head Gardener!

In Genesis we read that God himself planted a garden, watered it, and met his people there. In the fullness of time it was in a garden of olives that Jesus agonised so that 'his sweat was like drops of blood' as he faced crucifixion (Luke 22:39–44). It was also in a garden that, after his resurrection, he met and spoke to the weeping Mary of Magdala who then ran and told his incredulous disciples that he is alive again (John 20:15–18).

In our predominantly urban lives it is gardens, whether indoors, on a balcony, or outdoors, that keep us in touch with the basic, elemental rhythms of life. We have to observe the seasons, to dig at the digging time, plant each crop or flower at its optimum planting time, and not forget to bring the tender ones in again before the first frost of winter. There is indeed 'a time to plant and a time to uproot', not to mention 'a time for war' on slugs, snails and other pests, though in that respect I am not so sure of the complementary 'time for peace' (Ecc 3:2,8). Etched into a pane of glass in a window of the library at Montacute House, Somerset, is a Latin inscription by its first owner, Sir Edward Phelips, a late sixteenth-century Speaker of the House of Commons. Part of it is translated as:

> Do not scorn or grumble about this gentle toil;
> It is shared by the greatest gardener of all.
> Do not look for Him only amid the stars of
>   heaven:
> For it is in the ordinary things of life that you
>   may find God.

It is always a joy to watch over and care for plants that have been given to us as presents. They naturally tend to have a special place in the affections of the recipient because of this link with the donor. Often a prayer for the friend who gave each one arises spontaneously whenever one walks by, or stays to weed in the vicinity. For those who do not have a garden, or are not mobile enough to care for one, then a window box, tubs on the doorstep, or a collection of indoor plants give contact with the soil. Plants need watering, pruning of spent flowers, feeding and general nurturing; all activities that can be very much part of prayer.

Established gardens are so full of memories, and this aspect of gardening can be deliberately fostered. One couple who gardened on sandy soil where stones are scarce formed the habit of bringing back large ones from memorable holidays, and the sight of these stones as they moved around their garden frequently caused them to recall and give thanks for all those good times. Often particular stones would spark off a time of general praise and thanksgiving to God as they continued with their gardening tasks.

A friend of mine tells how she had for a long time gathered stones in her various world travels. The year her father died she made a bubble fountain area in her garden, symbolising the springs of living water he had spent his life taking to others.

A number of friends who came to the Service of Thanksgiving for his life brought stones from the many places throughout the globe where they had worked with him. The most poignant one was a piece of the Berlin Wall, brought by a German doctor who her father had led to the Lord when doing relief work in Berlin immediately after the Second World War. The doctor placed his bit of the wall among the other stones being bathed by the trickling water with the comment, 'Your father has been breaking down walls all his life'. The making of such a special place in a garden gives tangible expression to the many emotions that will be encountered following the deeply felt loss of the one

who is being commemorated.

The more routine gardening tasks are often an excellent opportunity to really get down to some intercession, perhaps in more detail than is possible at any other time. I will always be grateful for the seasoned gardener who often phones me up to ask what engagements I have coming up so that he can pray more meaningfully for me. He says he does not have to think a great deal when cutting a straight, uncomplicated hedge, and he likes to use the time spent on such tasks to pray specifically for people.

Everywhere you go in a garden there are reminders of the Creator. Chaucer called nature 'the vicar of th' Almightie Lord' and years later William Cowper observed that 'Nature is but a name for an effect whose cause is God'. There is just so much going on in a garden that recalls the teaching of Scripture, and this frequently prompts us to pray about the lessons learned. For instance, as one sows fiddly little seeds and wishes that they were easier to handle, thoughts might easily turn to the parable that Jesus told about the tiny mustard seed. It is so very small yet it grows into the largest garden plant, big enough for many birds to feed and roost there. If at the same time one is also grappling with some problem that seems just too great to tackle alone, this parable can be an encouragement to at least pitch in and make some contribution. Those tiny seeds might well prompt a very productive prayer time while working out there in the open.

Digging and preparing the soil ready for sowing naturally seems to prompt questions. These might run along the lines of: 'Is my life at this moment good, fertile, receptive soil for the seed of the Word of God to germinate in, or am I at present rather stony soil, giving a poor and disappointing yield?' The ever-present chore of keeping on top of garden weeds can prompt reflection on another parable told by Jesus. Weeds that are the cares of this world can choke the good seed of his Word before it can take hold and grow in our too-busy lives.

In fact, come to think of it, the thirteenth chapter of the Gospel of Matthew could very well be called the gardeners' chapter. It contains two other relevant parables, the one about an enemy sowing weed seeds after the farmer has sown his crops, and the one about the treasure buried in a field. Digging in the garden today can indeed bring out treasures from seed sown in the memory years ago.

The summer chore of watering can become a delightful occupation for it offers the chance to reflect on some of the many scriptural allusions to water. Jesus called the thirsty to drink 'living water', and promised that people could be channels of it too. Plants that are wilting in the sun might prompt me to ask myself if I really long for God with every fibre of my being, as the deer pants for water after a chase (Ps 42:1). I can supply the watery needs of my plants, but is my whole life like a well that supplies my own needs and those of others, or is it at the moment something of a 'broken cistern' (Jer 2:13)? There is also the teaching about giving a cup of cold water to those in need which prompts me to ask myself, and the Lord, whether I am being hospitable to those for whom he would have me care.

While there is almost always something to be done in a garden, just being out there invites one to slow down and look around in wonder. There will be something new to see, and often some fresh scent hanging in the air, that invites one to linger, and savour. Professor Louis Pasteur, the founder of modern microbiology and originator of the process of pasteurisation, wrote, 'The more I study nature, the more I am amazed at the creator'. A garden is a splendid place in which to slow down and recover the lost art of wondering, to let ourselves be amazed by what we see, and touch, and hear, and smell.

Bernard, the twelfth-century Abbot of the Cistercian monastery at Clairvaux in France, taught his monks to reflect on the natural world. He wrote, 'You will find something far greater in the woods than you will in books. Stones and trees will teach you what you can never learn from masters.' He also said, 'He who labours as he prays lifts his heart to God with his hands.' Unfortunately we have let ourselves get so busy, and allowed life to become so specialised and compartmentalised, that we make a false distinction between prayer and the routine tasks of the day.

'Lifting the heart to God' is a lovely definition of prayer. It encompasses all the wordless aspects that are often so hard to enter into, as well as the more familiar components like adoration, thanksgiving, confession and intercession. When one is working in a garden the heart can remain alert for the gentle whisper that is so often the presence of God, and for anything that he may choose to speak into our situation, while the body gets on with the routine tasks of the season.

Gardens are great places for mulling over the day or the week. Somehow they help one to rejoice and give thanks for all those things that have gone well, and they are conducive to getting the disappointments, frustrations and mistakes into some sort of perspective. Sometimes it is helpful to read a few verses of a psalm or a poem on which to focus one's thoughts before going out. One morning I had read Psalm 52 and verse eight was still resonating with me in the evening.

> But I am like an olive tree
>   flourishing in the house of God;
> I trust in God's unfailing love
>   for ever and ever.

Repeating it over and over to myself I soon found that each word had something to say to me. Even the first little word 'but' reminded me that over and above all the problems and distress in the world, armed robberies, homelessness, abject poverty, volcanic eruptions, earthquakes, floods and drought, there is more. God is somehow there, and he is here with me as I wrestle not only with the weeds but with the world.

Being 'like' an olive tree does not mean that I am one, but that I can flourish in the presence of the Lord. Trees have stability, they stay put. They do not migrate as some birds do, nor do they rush around as so many of us humans do. This led me on to reflect about why I am so often in a hurry and under pressure, then to some useful conclusions about how to reduce the pressure I put myself under, and to a few practical alterations I needed to make in my life. So I was able to work out some necessary lifestyle changes as well as getting on with tidying up the garden.

A garden always seems to me an appropriate place in which to confess failings and acknowledge wrong attitudes, thoughts and actions, and then to listen to what the Lord wants to say about it all. It is a great listening place. Just hearing the birdsong can remind us to delight more in the Lord, to cast our cares on to him, and even perhaps to take ourselves a little less seriously.

Gardens are often places that invite confidences. It may be that there is someone who really needs to be listened to, but who for various reasons finds it difficult to talk about their cares and burdens, especially in a structured and formal way. As you quietly and companionably get on with your gardening such a person may be able to unburden themselves in a way that neither of you might manage so well face to face. You can always stop what you are doing and give them your undivided attention, or take them in for a cuppa, or change to whatever else seems to be appropriate, as the conversation develops. Often it is then quite natural to include the Father more directly in the conversation, and to pray together.

Being in a garden seems to encourage spontaneous reflection. The very name of a flower can prompt one to slow down and reflect, instead of continuing to rush through the garden as one tends to rush through the rest of life. Heartsease. Now there's a name to make one ponder. The very sight of those cheerful little faces that seed themselves everywhere in my garden, is enough to make me smile as I pass by, and relax a little. They invite a response. If my heart is not at ease, then they are an invitation to linger and search out what is amiss. When all is well then I can smile back at them and go on my way encouraged, but I cannot pass them by and be unaffected by their presence.

Dandelions are another story. They are such a sunny, cheerful colour when in flower, and then come those entrancing, fluffy seed heads that so delight children but cause gardeners to despair. There are just too many of them, they take root everywhere and are almost impossible to eradicate. They are weeds precisely because they are so prolific and so tenacious. Their single long taproot tends to break off, and then it regenerates a whole new plant from the tiniest remnant. What a pity that something so beautiful becomes a nuisance because of its very exuberance. The cuckoo of the plant world, they insert themselves anywhere and their strength soon overcomes more delicate plants. As I root them out they sometimes remind me of my inclination to play the joker and to make facetious comments at inappropriate moments, indeed to overplay my hand just like the dandelion. There's nothing wrong with the inclination but it can be misused and out of place. Sometimes the sight of a dandelion moves me to pray about the various weeds in my life, which are sadly just as rampant and difficult to eradicate.

Gardens are often used for more formal and planned times of quiet reflection and prayer, as part of a team or church Awayday, or to facilitate an individual retreat. On one such day a friend of mine was wandering in the large garden of a house on the edge of a wood. The boundary between the garden and the wood was not always easy to find. It seemed to be marked in places by a wire strand fence and by there being some attempt to cut down the ever invasive bracken beyond. However the boundary with the adjacent property was easy to spot because of the contrasting, tamed orderliness of next door. All this set him reflecting on the state of his own inner boundaries, and of how he needed to maintain them better in order not to be engulfed by work. He realised that there was a danger he could become as completely taken over by the problems of other people, as the garden would be by the invading bracken unless it was deliberately and regularly cut back. His thoughts turned to prayer, and he then made some important and specific decisions about how to maintain his own personal boundaries, and so reduce the alarming pressure he had been under.

Another person wandering in the same garden was struck by the remains of many old bonfires dotted around the place. They were eloquent evidence of the unremitting battle to keep the garden from reverting to being a wild wood once more. This led her to reflect on the graphic picture of God sitting at the refiner's fire, patiently lifting gold and silver free from the dross in which it was encrusted (Mal 3:3; Zech 13:9).

The apostle Paul also uses good gardening illustrations. When rebuking divisions in the church and calling for co-operation rather than competition, he writes 'I planted the seed, Apollos watered it, but God made it grow. So neither he who plants nor he who waters is anything, but only God, who makes things grow' (1 Cor 3:6,7). Seed planting, weeding, watering and harvesting; looking on nature and learning spiritual lessons from it, all are there in a garden, and waiting to be turned into prayer. As C.S. Lewis wrote: '**All ground is holy and every bush** (could we but see it) **a Burning Bush.**'

Be Creative

1. Make a miniature garden in a bowl, seed tray or large jar. Group houseplants together to form an indoor jungle, oasis or forest. Use all aspects of nurturing your creation as prayer.

2. Find some fixture in your garden, a tree or shrub, a seat or an ornament, that will remind you of those for whom you want to pray regularly. If necessary buy or construct something specially for selected people in your life. Once a day pause as you pass 'their' object and lift them into the presence of the Lord.

3. Whenever you go out to garden let your thoughts be on God, the Creator. See yourself as co-operating with him in your particular patch of earth, even if it is only a window box. As you go about your gardening tasks let your thoughts wander; follow them; consider and reflect. Laugh at any absurdities you find, and share your joke with the Lord who also once walked upon this earth.

5

Music in Prayer

*It is good to praise the LORD and make music
to your name, O Most High.
(Psalm 92:1)*

Music is universal. Go outside and listen to the
birds singing, the breeze rustling in the trees or the
sound of running water, and know that all nature
is making music. The psalmist recognises this in
Psalm 148: 'Praise him, sun and moon, praise him,
all you shining stars . . . you highest heavens and
you waters above the skies . . . you great sea creatures and all ocean depths, lightning and hail,
snow and clouds, stormy winds . . . mountains and
all hills . . . wild animals . . . flying birds . . . Let
them praise the name of the LORD. Psalm 98, too,
says 'Let the sea resound, and everything in it . . .
Let the rivers clap their hands, let the mountains
sing together for joy; let them sing before the LORD'
(vv 7 & 9). I often think of this walking with my dog
in the early morning. I deliberately 'tune in' to the
music of the sea, the wind and the gulls, and join in
the praise to our Creator and Lord.

People have made music down the centuries and
throughout the world, using various languages and

instruments producing totally different sounds. Music somehow touches feelings and souls and expresses things that are beyond words. It is used in almost all religions and has always played a significant part in Judaistic and Christian worship. Exodus chapter 15 tells how the Lord had just saved the Israelites from the Egyptians, bringing them miraculously through the Red Sea. Then Moses and the people took time to sing a song of praise to the Lord, recounting all his exploits. Not only that, but they brought on the dancing girls. We read in verses 20 and 21:

> Then Miriam the prophetess, Aaron's sister, took a tambourine in her hand, and all the women followed her, with tambourines and dancing. Miriam sang to them:
>
>> Sing to the LORD,
>>   for he is highly exalted.
>> The horse and its rider
>>   he has hurled into the sea.

It was rather amazing that, in the midst of all the rush and excitement of the night before the great escape, they remembered to pack their tambourines! Singing to the Lord must have been a regular and important part of their worship, and they expected to do so in the future. I wonder what you and I would have packed if we had to suddenly leave our homes?

In Judges 5:3 Deborah, too, says 'I will sing to the LORD, I will sing; I will make music to the LORD'. Over and over again in the Psalms we are exhorted to 'Make music to the Lord'. David, himself, must have beer a very skilful musician, and playing the harp was part of his regular activity. 1 Samuel 18:10 tells us, 'David was playing the harp, as he usually did'. It must have been very soothing and God-centred playing, if it had the effect of making Saul 'feel better' when troubled by an evil spirit (1 Sam 16:23). I wonder if he took his harp with him when he was out on the hillside looking after his sheep? I can imagine him sitting there composing and singing Psalm 23, and many of his psalms seem like listening in to his private prayer.

A friend of mine who plays the guitar and piano, often sits with her guitar in her personal prayer times, and lets her hands move over the strings, making music spontaneously from the soul. She says it may start as something conscious that she wants to express, or it may be a matter of tuning in to something so deep that she is hardly aware of it. So she may find herself expressing a sudden rush of joy or sorrow. On occasion the music itself (on guitar or piano) becomes the prayer, a tool for expression. Words may come which express the feeling or desire, or the voice may be used without words.

Sometimes we may not feel like praying, we may be a little 'out of sorts', and the simple making of music brings us into the presence of the Lord. It is

Pam Dodson.

wonderful for relieving stress and is healing in
various ways. It is often in music that the Holy
Spirit will speak back to us, or interpret what we
have expressed in some way. Even the rhythm
itself seems to play a significant part. Rhythm is in
our very nature. Starting with our heartbeat in the
womb, rhythm is part of our physiology. People who
are tone-deaf can still appreciate rhythm, and even
people who are profoundly deaf can sense it. My
friend finds she can also use music in intercession.
On one occasion she had a heart concern for a deaf
person who was having a nervous breakdown. She
was singing to the Lord and having a sense of holding this person in her arms like a baby, singing a
soothing lullaby to him, as if being a channel of

God's love. Two days later she heard he had made a remarkable recovery.

Somehow music whether it is made by nature, ourselves, or somebody else, seems to bless and invigorate us. Not everybody can play an instrument. I can't, although I love to sing and greatly enjoy harmonising in a choir. Harmony, whether orchestral or voice, somehow reminds me of nature as God intended it to be, a foretaste of that time when God will 'bring all things in heaven and on earth together under one head, even Christ' (Eph 1:10). You can also 'make music in your heart to the Lord' as it says in Ephesians 5:19. Some people play music on a tape or CD, as part of their worship. As I got up one morning I put on the *Gloria* tape by John Rutter. The lively passage at the beginning made me feel excited for the day, then as I had a bath I played the more peaceful passages and relaxed in God's love. By the time I arrived at the Celtic blessing of peace I was ready to sit at my prayer desk and read the Bible. At the end of my prayer time I played the lovely blessing from Numbers that comes at the end of the tape: 'The Lord bless you and keep you'. I took that blessing into the day.

There is so much wonderful sacred music, too, that is an aid to worship. The ancient Plainsong or Gregorian chant, with its simple, repetitive phrases and cadences, seems to carry one right into the presence of God. It is interesting that the CDs and cassettes of monks singing the Gregorian Plainsong have become so popular recently, even with non-Christians. The music speaks to the human spirit, although the Latin words may not be understood. Also finding fresh popularity among Christian and non-Christian, is the chanted music of the tenth-century German nun, Hildegard of Bingen. At the age of forty-three she had a vision of flames from heaven alighting upon her, with the message that she was to write music that would allow others to share her spiritual experiences. Princess Diana's funeral awakened many to the haunting music of John Tavener. He and Arvo Part are two contemporary composers who have become more popular in the last decade and whose musical styles are deeply rooted in Orthodox and medieval liturgy.

The black American spirituals are timeless as are many of the old hymns. It is sometimes helpful to sit with a hymn book open during prayer time, finding a hymn to sing which expresses what we want to say to the Lord. Many of the modern hymns and choruses are lovely too, especially as they are often addressed to the Lord, and are not just about him. Taizé, in France, has for many years now been a centre for a remarkable work of the Lord. Thousands gather there from all over the world, most of them young people, but all ages are represented. Worship centres round the distinctive singing. This is very repetitive and chant-like, but it soars and dips in a way that carries the participants into the presence of the Lord. Taizé music is available on tape and CD and can be obtained in most Christian bookshops.

Some of the most 'heavenly' music I have ever heard was in Darmstardt, in Germany, where the Mary sisters were having a Welcoming ceremony for some new sisters. The choir was arranged in a semi-circle on the platform, and near the beginning, they suddenly broke into 'singing in the Spirit'. While doing this they each moved forward and presented a thorny twig to the entrants, signifying the crown of thorns. Then towards the end of the ceremony, each one drew a new sister into their circle, presenting them with a flower. While they did this, they again spontaneously broke into 'singing in the Spirit', with the most beautiful harmonies and cadences. It was truly 'out of this world'. Paul says in 1 Corinthians 14:15 'I will sing with my spirit, but I will also sing with my mind'. Music will often express more than we can in words, so let us follow Paul's example.

Oratorios, such as the *Messiah* have blessed countless people, whether they are taking part or just listening. As a teenager I was attending a Christian camp in Malvern. We had a day's outing to Worcester, and went into the Cathedral when the famous soprano, Isobel Bailie, was practising for a performance of the *Messiah* in the evening. As we sat quietly, we listened to her magnificent voice soaring up to the rafters singing 'I know that my Redeemer lives'. If I had not already known it, I'm sure I would have realised then that my Redeemer does indeed live.

John Caroe wrote:

Many composers (and artists) have the ability to express the inexpressible across the range of human emotions . . . a portrayal of vistas with the beauty of eternity, quite independently above and beyond the human condition. Such music speaks life and hope into our souls because in listening to it we sense that we touch a source of truth, security and wisdom.[1]

There is no reason why we shouldn't use secular music either in our praying. Whatever our taste in music, some will sound lively, some sad, some dramatic and some peaceful. In playing or listening to different moods we can tune in to our own needs or those of others and turn them into prayer, praise or intercession. In fact, in doing so, we may lift a dark mood, or find that a difficulty doesn't seem so hard after all. Music is often used in therapy with both children and adults. As the therapist tunes in to the feelings of the individual, the person feels himself understood and valued, and so gains confidence.

When the people of Judah were totally surrounded and outnumbered by their enemies, Jehoshaphat, according to God's instructions,

appointed men to sing to the LORD and to praise him for the splendour of his holiness as they went out at the head of the army, saying:

'Give thanks to the LORD,
  for his love endures forever.'

> As they began to sing and praise, the LORD set ambushes against the men . . . and they were defeated.
>
> (2 Chron 20:21–22)

So the people of Judah did not have to fight, but see the deliverance of the Lord. That can happen to us too when we trust the Lord, not with an unrealistic triumphalism, but with faith in a God who keeps his promises. When facing a difficult situation, to make music and sing to the Lord, may or may not change the circumstances, but it will certainly change our attitude to them.

As Joyce Critchlow says:

> There is a Russian saying: To sing is to pray twice. Certainly it is harder for the mind to wander when singing. We use more energy, so we're giving God more of ourselves. Heart singing (joying, praying, even crying at times) can be as much tuning in to God as physical singing. There are many times when singing is difficult: in sickness, sadness or worry, the muscles governing our singing seize up. It's then that we can sing psalms, hymns and spiritual songs in our hearts to God (Col 3:16).[2]

The Psalms are meant to be sung and sometimes it is good to sing through one making up our own simple tune. It doesn't matter if we are tone-deaf, God will hear and read our hearts. Psalm 33:2,3, says

'Praise the LORD with the harp; make music to him on the ten-stringed lyre. Sing to him a new song; play skilfully and shout for joy.' We may not be able to do the former, although we can appreciate another's skill. We can all, however, shout for joy. The psalm goes on to give reasons for doing so. We can surely do the same, as we look round at creation and look back on our lives. At the end the psalmist recognises that death and famine are realities, and today there are plenty of dreadful things happening, but we can wait and hope in God's unfailing love. A good exercise is to write a personal psalm, perhaps recalling God's goodness, even in dark days, making up a simple tune or using a familiar one. It doesn't have to be brilliant poetry as long as we 'sing it' from the heart and it articulates what we really feel. God knows and understands our feelings and he loves to hear us express them.

There are various examples of modern psalms in print, but to show that anyone can profitably pray in this way, here is a very private sample, written at a retreat.

God Came

I wept in the dark, but my tears were within.
I screamed on the inside, making no noise,
Too frightened to fear, just gritting my teeth
I beat on the bars that were keeping me in.

God came in the darkness and brought me light.

Thank you God, for giving me sight.

I struggled outside, now using my feet.
It wasn't so hard, once I got on the road.
The scream was still there, only dimly recalled,
The screaming of others more loud in my ear.

God came in the darkness and brought me light.
Thank you God, for giving me sight.

I ran and ran to catch up in time,
So much to do that was needed and fine.
My scream was forgotten for most of the time,
For life was exciting and challenging too.

God came in the darkness and brought me light.
Thank you God, for giving me sight.

But one day it halted and everything changed.
Familiar scenes were all gone in a trice,
A new ground beneath me which caused me to
  stop.
The scream that was in me came up to the top.

God came in the darkness and brought me light.
Thank you God, for giving me sight.

The bars of my cell were all crumbling and loose.
The way was made open to recognise me.
The scream was let out, when the Spirit came in,
Where He most felt at home, within the real me.

God came in the darkness and gave me wings,
I'm flying away and my heart it now sings.

It is easy to let life hurry by without taking time to reflect on what is happening. Spending time singing and making music to the Lord is one way of glorifying him, and lifting our own spirits.

Of course, making music, as with other creative activities, does not, of itself, make us better Christians. As Graham Kendrick says in his book *Christian Music*:

> How foolish we are if we think the beauty of the prayers, songs and music, or the dignity or solemnity of religious services in themselves, please God. After all, He can call upon countless angels to offer Him incredible worship beyond our imaginations! No, God is looking for a deeper kind of music, a richer kind of liturgy. He listens for the music of obedience, and the daily liturgy of justice and righteousness in the way we affect the society round us.[3]

Suggestions for Prayer Activity

1. Go for a walk in the countryside, park or garden. Deliberately listen to the music of nature and join in with the worship, in your heart.

2. Play a recording of music you like, whether sacred or secular. Allow the Holy Spirit to prompt you in praise, worship or intercession. A lively passage may lead you to sing along in thankfulness. A peaceful melody gives you an

opportunity to absorb the Lord's peace, and pray for people you know who are in need of it. A sad part may help you to tune in to your own or other's sadness, and pray for God's comfort.

3. If you play an instrument at all, try letting your hands improvise and express the feelings and desires of your heart.

4. Sing through a psalm that expresses what you want to say, not worrying about how it sounds. God will appreciate it.

5. Write your own psalm, tuning in honestly to your real feelings and recollections, and see if a tune, also, comes to you.

6

Movement and Dance in Prayer

Let them praise his name with dancing.
(Psalm 149:3)

Dancing is a natural expression of joy. A grandmother I know had a telephone call to say that a long awaited grandchild had arrived, so she hurried round to tell a friend the good news. Although the friend was in her eighties, she immediately seized her and together they whirled round the kitchen in a joyful dance. How lovely that they felt free to do that spontaneously. Often we are too inhibited to express ourselves with our bodies, although, in fact we are always making non-verbal communication without realising it. People in Old Testament times suffered from no such inhibitions. As early as Exodus 15:20 we learn that Miriam played the tambourine and danced. David, too, danced before the Lord (2 Sam 6:14) and was wrongly criticised for it. Even God has been depicted as dancing his pleasure. The Jerusalem Bible translation of Zephaniah 3:17 says, 'He will dance with shouts of joy for you', and to this day, dancing forms a very real part of Jewish worship. Nature, too, can be described as dancing. Angela Hardcastle, the dancer and choreographer, once put it like this:

The beauties of nature lie not only in colour and sound, texture and perfume, but also in motion. To see long grass blowing in the wind, antelopes leaping, a seagull gliding or a boiling sea breaking on rocks is to know for sure that God invented movement. The Great Lover is also the Great Dancer. It follows that man, created by God in His image, with a mind and a spirit capable of conscious love and worship, has potentially the greatest beauty of movement and expression in the created world.[1]

There is a concept of life itself being a dance. The constant movement, the interweaving, the changes of form and colour, different characters coming and going and the varieties of scene, can all be described as dance. This idea comes in some of our very old carols, such as one that says, 'Tomorrow shall be my dancing day'. In this, the Son of God says that the purpose of his incarnation is 'to call my true love [i.e. mankind] to my dances'. Also in more recent days, Sydney Carter reflects on the life of Christ with 'I danced in the morning'. His idea of Christ as 'Lord of the Dance' is another way of portraying him as Lord of Life. His promise to 'lead you all in the dance' is an assurance of Christ's desire to lead all who will follow him, through all the experiences of their lives. It finishes 'I'll live in you if you'll live in me; I am the Lord of the dance, said he.'

Human beings have danced since the beginning of time, and in every tribe and nation. However these dances are most often arranged and traditional. Spontaneous dancing is not so common, although children often do it without embarassment. In recent days, movement of the body as an expression of prayer and worship is more commonly used in churches than it used to be, where people have the freedom to do so.

Even the simple raising of hands in praise can be very meaningful, if it is a heartfelt action and not done automatically. The Psalms often talk about lifting up hands in praise, such as in Psalm 63:4, 'In your name I will lift up my hands'. Many times in the Bible, too, people are described as falling on their faces before the Lord. Even Jesus 'fell with his face to the ground and prayed' in Gethsemane.

It has been said that in ordinary conversation, words count for only seven per cent of the overall communication. The tone and volume of our voice accounts for thirty-eight per cent and body language and facial expression fifty-five per cent. It is not surprising, therefore, that people find that using their bodies to express their feelings in prayer to God, somehow emphasises what they want to say and makes it more meaningful. I am not just thinking of celebration and praise but also of other expressions, such as longing or petition.

There are times, too, when we do not feel like praying, and simple body movements can lift our spirits. I am not a natural dancer, but do sometimes find that movement is helpful in my personal prayer time. One day, feeling rather depressed and deflated, after having received some criticism of my work, I felt like curling up in a ball. I sat on a low chair and did just that, being aware that God knew how I felt and wanted to lift up my head. As I experienced his love pouring into me I gradually uncurled. In the end I was standing up with my arms raised, praising the Lord. The mere fact of going through the physical movements drew my spirit into an experience of restoration. Sometimes I extend my arms and hands forwards and upwards to indicate my openness to God and anything he may say to me. This seems to strengthen my resolve to be open. At other times I might turn my hands palm down on my knees as I leave my concerns with him. Then I turn my hands palm upwards to receive strength, guidance, wisdom or whatever is needed to deal with those matters. When anxious or afraid it helps sometimes to clench the hands tightly and observe how much energy is used up being tense. Then slowly uncurl the hands, at the same time releasing the anxiety to the Lord.

On occasion, I have put a worship song on the tape recorder and gently danced round the room, expressing the meaning of the song in simple movements. It helps me to praise the Lord with my whole being. After all, we are exhorted to offer our bodies to God as a living sacrifice (Rom 12:1) and the first and greatest commandment is to love God with all our mind and soul and strength. Sometimes worshipping with the body helps to concentrate the mind on him. We are whole people, body, mind and spirit; what we do with one part affects the whole of us. When we are able to express ourselves in movement and dance, it often results in the release of something much deeper. Sometimes a kind of psychological knot that we are hardly conscious of, becomes 'untied' under the ministry of the Holy Spirit.

One of my friends often uses movement in her private praying, and finds it brings her in touch with deep insights, unreached by speech or imagination. On one occasion, at a retreat centre, she remembers going into a large room in the dark, carrying a candle. She had strapped a walkman to her waist, and put earphones on, so that no one was disturbed, and she 'danced with the Lord'. Sometimes she was moving away, sometimes towards, sometimes following, sometimes alongside the Lord. All this found deep echoes in her heart. She also says that expressing a story or prayer from Scripture in movement, helps her to get in touch with its deeper meaning. She remembers finding it helpful to express Paul's wonderful prayer in Ephesians 3:14–21 in movement only, mainly arm movements on this occasion. Another time she acted out the story of Abraham and Isaac and realised that Abraham being an old man and Isaac a strong lad, Isaac must have acquiesced in following God's instructions.

Several years ago she felt moved to act out Mary anointing the feet of Jesus. As she knelt at the feet of Jesus, she found she could not raise her eyes to look him in the face. This led her to look into her heart to discover why that was. Some years later she went through the same exercise, and found to her joy, that she could look him in the face and was overwhelmed by his love.

More and more, nowadays, dance groups are being formed in fellowships and churches. They find that while meeting and praying together, the Holy Spirit guides them to develop movements which are a blessing to them and to the people who may subsequently watch them. The group itself will often be blessed in doing this without an audience. In fact, if a dance is going to be performed in public, it should be of the highest quality. One of my friends who has used dance for many years, and for a long time led a small group, expresses it like this:

> There are many kinds of Christian dance. Some powerfully depict the meaning of the actual words of song or Scripture. Some show our response to life's hurts and the freedom Christ can bring. Some depict a heart response of joy and worship with no particular words. For me personally, I feel an inner release of spiritual worship, which can be more meaningful than just speech. There can also be an element of outreach, to draw others together into deeper worship from the heart. It is essential that this is a response of my heart first, and not an end in itself. It is a non-verbal language that can interpret the meaning of the words with a powerful impact. Sometimes we get used to words and using movement brings them to life again. Proclaiming the Name of Jesus calls for a response expressed in movement, and this helps me to live it out in daily life.

This friend sometimes uses flags in the fellowship she attends and points out that all through history, flags have been used for proclamation as well as providing identity and a rallying point. Why not use them in proclaiming that 'Jesus is King'? She tells how in a recent service several people marched round the hall waving flags as they sang 'Tell it loud, tell it long, tell the world what God has done'. She is able to proclaim the supremacy of Jesus higher, more widely, more visibly, and more joyously with a flag as an extension of her arm.

She goes on to describe attending a week's seminar held by the Sacred Dance Group, and clearly remembers the evening presentation given in church. It represented the Fruit of the Spirit, and the effect it had on her was unforgettable.

For PEACE two dancers, dressed in blue, danced together in perfect harmony.

Depicting there were several dancers in white and yellow, running up the centre and round the chancel. 'They were spilling out joy to us from their hands, as they came. As I was in the front row, I kept receiving joy each time'.

To show LOVE they dressed in white with red capes. The dance was not choreographed, but with prayer for the inspiration of the Holy Spirit they danced in pairs. One depicted a troubled person and the other came to comfort her. At last she took her by one hand, and with the other she pointed upwards to Jesus. She then took her red cloak and gently held it round her for protection, showing the love of Jesus. My friend says 'This happened over twenty years ago, but I can still "see it".'

Another friend wrote this poem to describe how she felt about 'dancing her prayer':

I've found a joy, oh such a joy,
I know the Lord is in it,
For He has opened up the way,
Enabled me to reach and say,
This is the feeling that I have
For Jesus' life has made me glad.
And so I reach out arms to you.
My hands stretch up for blessings new.
And in the movement up and high
I loose myself – I touch the sky.
I know my Lord is really there.
I feel His love, His peace, His care.

Why should this be, I do not know
Why moving helps my praise to flow.
And yet it does, and looking round,
Faces reveal the joy they've found.
And as we move in one accord,
We symbolise your oneness, Lord.[2]

Sue Sutherland, in her little book '*With All that Is Within*' says that dance or movement in prayer confirms what our minds and hearts are saying.

> An action will fix and seal what has already begun to happen in our minds and spirits, in the same way as writing our thoughts down on paper fixes them. A physical action will make them more real, and thus confirm to the Lord that we are committed and serious about what we are saying. There is an old Chinese Proverb

that says 'I hear and forget, I see and remember, I do and I understand'. Our body language can say as much to God as our minds or voices.[3]

When we are using movement or dance in our own private prayer time, nobody but God sees it. If it helps us to enter more fully into praise and worship, then it is worth pursuing. It may well lead us into new insights, as we respond to the Holy Spirit.

If we belong to a group and wish to make a dance presentation in public, then it needs to be done with great integrity, care and sensitivity. That will take much preparation, practice and prayer.

Some worry that there is an unwholesome sexual connotation to dance and this can happen. Dance has been misused, as with Herodias' daughter in Matthew 14:6–8. We are 'whole' people and sexuality is part of being human, which we show in so many ways, mostly unconsciously. However, when dance is performed carefully and prayerfully, there is no reason why it should be provocative or offensive. Clothing needs to be appropriate and women often wear long skirts. Let everything be done for the glory of God, and not for self-advertisement.

Other people have reservations about dance in church, feeling that it is inappropriate. However, nowadays there is more acceptance that we are creative human beings. The creative spark is given to us by God and dance is one expression of it. But we must take care not to force dance on a reluctant congregation.

There are various seminars and workshops available to those who wish to learn more about Christian dance, such as those arranged by the Christian Dance Fellowship of Britain. People attending these have often found their own prayer and worship enhanced by the things they have experienced there. Some, too, have been able to start their own ance group as a result.

Suggestions for Prayer Activity

1. Use simple movements in your personal prayer to emphasise the feeling or desire that you want to bring to the Lord, e.g. lying flat on your face in repentance or submission; raising the arms in praise; holding palms upwards to receive what you need for the day.

2. Act out a particular story or prayer from Scripture, using movement only. You can also do this using only hand and arm movements.

3. Put on a tape recording or CD of a worship song and make up a dance that seems illustrate it, as the Holy Spirit leads you.

4. If you discover one or two friends who are also interested in Christian dance, get with them and prayerfully arrange some dance movements illustrating a song or Bible story. You will be blessed in the doing of it yourselves, and in time

Christian
Dance Fellowship
of
Britain

you may become skilled enough to perform in public.

If you wish to learn more, contact the Christian Dance Fellowship of Britain, 25 Scardale Crescent, Scarborough, North Yorkshire, YO12 6LA, and ask for information about their Conferences and Seminars.

Praise the Lord, all you servants of the Lord
who minister by night in the house of the Lord.
Lift up your hands in the sanctuary
and praise the Lord.
May the Lord, the Maker of heaven and earth,
bless you from Zion.
(Psalm 134)

7

Praying with Pictures

Groans that words cannot express.
(Romans 8:26)

The aim of art, according to Aristotle, 'is to represent not the outward appearance of things, but their inward significance'. Many of us know times when we struggle to come to grips with an inward significance of which we are only dimly aware and certainly cannot articulate. At times like this it can be helpful to doodle, to twiddle and experiment, rather than to set out to draw a definable something.

The aim is to undertake a private exploration, not to produce a finished picture suitable to hang on the wall for all to see. It is an attempt to express the otherwise inexpressible, a growing and evolving assertion of something that is emerging from within, rather than a well thought out composition. It is a statement that cannot be packaged into words, an attempt to begin to apprehend an inward significance.

I tend to think of doodling, drawing and painting as capable of being the visible counterpart to those times when 'the Spirit helps us in our weakness.

We do not know what we ought to pray, but the Spirit himself intercedes for us with groans that words cannot express'. The Amplified New Testament puts its, 'unspeakable yearnings and groanings too deep for utterance' Rom 8:26).

Making marks on paper, and allowing them to evoke memories, disappointments and desires, is just another way, a 'right brain' way, of praying. Letting those abstract marks bring situations, thoughts and feelings into focus, and exploring with God what is going on in the wordless depths of our being, is an additional way of entering into prayer.

You don't have to be an artist to pray this way, nor to have any particular artistic leanings. You do, however, need to be prepared to overcome some of those inhibitions most of us acquire about 'doing art', and to have a go. You will need to suspend all judgement about the aesthetic or utilitarian value of anything you may produce, and start making marks on paper. Any marks, any scrap paper, just get going. Allow what happens just to appear on the paper before you. Do not try to understand it, simply let it appear. Forget all those admonitions you have heard about a drawing needing to be recognisable as something in particular. This is a declaration of groanings and yearnings that express more truly than words can, all the chaos and confusion, the longings and desires, the joys and sorrows milling around within.

Some people find that they loosen up more and

are able to start representing their inner landscape on paper when they use their non-dominant hand. Making broad marks on large paper using thick chalks, crayons, pastels, charcoal or a large paint-brush is also a good way to get going. This helps to guard against the tendency to try and control or direct what may emerge. It is important to just let the marks, images and colours appear and mingle, portraying inner yearnings and longings that may previously have been pushed out of awareness in the general business of life.

Entering into this way of expression requires that one temporarily suspends critical thought and judgement. The essence of this approach is to become free for a while from the constraints and restraints that we all acquire in life, in order to take a look through a different lens. Looking at the same things from another angle brings out other highlights and shadows, encouraging one to take a fresh look at familiar things.

Portraying some aspect of your situation in this non-verbal way may enable you to notice connec-tions between facets of your life that you have so far not recognised. Sometimes it can graphically reveal the current effect of previous life experi-ences. I remember one woman who drew a tree to show how she was experiencing her life at that time. The branches were almost all in full leaf but the tree trunk was tightly enclosed in tall iron rail-ings. The tree had a good root system but adequate nourishment did not always reach the unfolding

94

areas of her life because of those railings. Discussion of this eventually prompted her to look again at influences from her early life that were originally designed to be protective, but which in adult life had become restrictive, and were now preventing her further growth. Once the drawing had brought this so vividly to her attention she was able to bring the matter into her prayers.

Looking at symbols that appear in doodles can sometimes reveal hidden attitudes that need attention. I remember one tedious meeting, during a rather prolonged reply to a contentious proposal, where several committee members were doodling on their agenda papers. For one, a doodle turned into an unmistakable gibbet, then a figure appeared suspended from the noose. His neighbour noticed this and later helped him look at some of his personal feelings about the long-winded speaker that were colouring his judgement and interfering with his ability to make an objective appraisal of the actual proposal.

Painting is a wonderful way of simplifying a complicated, jumbled mass into just the essential areas, the main topics, and disciplining oneself not to be distracted by the inclusion of irrelevant detail. No subject is impossible. Some are more difficult than others, but all can be tackled in one form or another. The object of the painting can so often become the subject of prayer, a sort of reminiscent, on-going, intermittent conversation and communication with God who is in us, as well as above and all around us. He is in the process of the painting, as well as in the subject matter, and in the painter.

Once when I was intrigued by a new subject, I was nearly deterred from having a go at it because I could find no convenient place in which to sit and sketch. Eventually I managed to perch my stool on a patch of discarded rubble that lay on the edge of a nettle patch. I was looking from bright sunshine into the interior of a shed and at first I could see little apart from a large yellow drainage hose, snaking out of the open doorway. Everything else seemed to be in almost total darkness. As I continued to gaze, I noticed just a glimmer of light here and there. Slowly these manifested themselves as a dimly-lit compartment at the back of the shed and a shaft of light on one rafter. Soon I could also make out the handle of a cultivator and the wheel of a bicycle, and then more of the machines and some other contents of the shed became visible. The more I looked the more I saw.

As I painted I was vaguely aware of parallels with my life and with life in general. The estate gardener came back and forth with his trailer of hedge clippings, sometimes pausing to nod and smile, and inevitably once to pose facetiously. Before leaving for the day he came round to see what I'd done, and remarked, 'Come again, you've tidied it up'. Of course I had had to focus on the things that caught my attention, and to leave out some incidental items, as well as much of the debris. I could not include all the bits and pieces blown in by the wind, and which were of no real consequence to the purpose of the shed, or the composition of my painting.

Later, as I reflected on my day, I realised how prayer can so often be a 'tidying up' of life, an examination of the contents that have accumulated in the shed of my life. Every so often I have needed to stop and reflect on the main purpose, the focus of my life at the stage I have just reached, sorting out the wheat from the chaff, discarding things that have merely blown in on the wind but which do not really contribute to current aims and intentions.

Painting is an act of faith, and it is full of surprises. Often we have to let go of preconceived ideas of what is 'right', and attend to the perceptions of the moment. We plan to capture a mood or a scene, or to portray an object in a particular way, and then find that it captures us, and takes over. The end result so often turns out to be somewhat different from the way we had expected it to go. Prayer also cannot be preplanned and controlled. It is a conversation and we are 'in charge' of only one side of it.

One day I was listening to someone who had been trying out the use of imagination in prayer. She reported that she had been having a dialogue with the Lord about a particular concern and said in a somewhat annoyed and dismayed tone, 'But that was not how the conversation was supposed to go'.

Before starting to pray she had mapped out in her mind both what she wanted to say, and what she expected to hear in reply. As so often happens the prayer conversation turned along rather different lines from her plan and her expectation.

A painter always has to learn about the medium he is using. Oil paints, acrylics, pastels and gouache each have their own individual properties and characteristics. The painter can only work with and through the qualities of the specific medium he is using. Water colour in particular cannot be precisely controlled and the outcome can never be absolutely predicted. This to me is an excellent reminder that however hard I try in various subtle ways I cannot control God. Of course I do not consciously set out to control him, but on reflection I sometimes realise with something of a shock that this has been the presumption behind my attitude and my petition.

At times a drawing or a painting may become the focus of prayer some little while after it was actually completed. On holidays I generally have a go at sketching whatever is in front of me, whenever we take a refreshment break. Coffee shops, pubs and cafes are chosen more for the view they afford than for the excellence of their cuisine! On the last evening of a week in the Lake District we did not wish to go far and what was before me were a few uninspiring local houses backed by the mighty Skiddaw rising steeply behind them. I had to hurry to get the scene into my sketchbook because the sun was setting, the light was continuously changing and the shadows which were my principle interest were elusive. Drawing made me look carefully, and it imprinted the scene on my mind and in my soul.

Some days later when I was praying, that picture came to mind, and I realised that my life is like the scene I had been observing on the last night of our holiday. Parts are open and catch the sun, other parts are in shade, dark and deeply mysterious. Some areas are almost permanently in shadow, others only fleetingly darkened. The pattern changes. As I reflected on certain issues going on for me at that time, I was able to pray around the subject of what I perceived to be shadow-forming clouds in my life, keeping the warmth and colour of the sunshine out of some areas. That sketch, done at the time for no other reason than the sheer enjoyment of doing it and as a good memory of the holiday, some while later became a graphic vehicle for prayer.

Art has been used to convey religious themes in one form or another since man first held a tool in his hands. It ranges from ancient and somewhat primitive cave drawings to modern paintings full of atmosphere and studied detail. Because we are all so different, art speaks to some more than to others, and often at different stages of their journey through life, so if it has not yet been part of your interest in life it is always worth giving it a try.

We need to remember that art was the only

teaching available to the majority of people for many hundreds of years while illiteracy was the norm. In our sophistication we have largely forgotten how to use it creatively. In the tradition of Eastern Churches, icons are still much used today. They are stylised and often lavishly decorated representations, sometimes carvings but more often paintings, of a sacred person, that have themselves come to be regarded as sacred objects. I have watched villagers in Cyprus approach icons around the walls of an otherwise bare little church on a remote hill, and have observed what an aid to worship they can be.

Taking time to really look at a great painting, spending time to gaze at it while allowing yourself to be drawn into the scene can be a wonderful prayer experience. Use the picture imaginatively so that the characters come alive for you. Let yourself become aware of the reality of the relationships between them. Let their hopes, fears, antagonisms and longings reveal themselves, as they might with a meditative reading of a story from the Gospels. Allow some aspect of the picture to resonate with something that is pertinent for you, some concern in your life at this time. Let it evoke what it will and let that be the focus of your prayer.

Henri Nouwen, a Dutch priest, Harvard professor and acclaimed writer, became captivated by a poster reproduction of Rembrandt's painting, entitled *The Return of the Prodigal Son*. After some years of living with it, and gazing at it, and a visit to see the original in St Petersburg in Russia, he wrote:

I felt drawn by the intimacy between the two figures, the warm red of the man's cloak, the golden yellow of the boy's tunic, and the mysterious light engulfing them both. But, most of all, it was the hands – the old man's hands – as they touched the boy's shoulders *that reached me in a place where I had never been reached before.* (my italics)[1]

He said of the painting that it 'had revealed to me the deepest longings of my heart'.

Nine years after first seeing that poster, and frequently speaking about what had rapidly become 'his' painting, he wrote a book with the same title. In this he examines the Scripture parable that evoked the painting, and the parallels he found between what he saw in Rembrandt's picture of it and the things he was becoming aware of in his own life. He concluded that, 'All of the Gospel is there. All of my life is there . . . The painting has become a mysterious window through which I can step into the Kingdom of God.'

Of course it is not just great classic masterpieces that can be used as the gateway to prayer. There are many books available with masterly illustrations, both paintings and photographs, often accompanied by written meditations or verses of Scripture, that are designed to be used as a focus for prayer. Some like to use them regularly, for others they are likely to be more of an occasional means into prayer, perhaps on holiday or as part of a day set aside for quiet reflection.

Be Creative

1. Take time to be quiet before God, then take up a pencil or paint brush and begin to make marks on paper. You do not even need a sheet of pristine new paper; the back of a cereal packet, card, wrapping paper – any surface will do, and any instrument. Felt tip pens and children's crayons are useful because they make clear, bold marks and come in a variety of colours and textures. You can even do as Jesus did and draw in the mud or the sand at your feet. This is especially useful if you are shy about beginning to use this method, and want your effort to be easily erased! Whether or not your marks portray recognisable objects, be aware of the process itself, of whatever thoughts, feelings and valuable memories it arouses. God created the right half of your brain as well as the left, and you are now allowing this part of your being to communicate with your Creator.

2. Choose a postcard, photograph or picture in a book that is meaningful to you, or of which you are particularly fond. Hold it in your hands, or place it before you, in a comfortable position. Recall that you are in the presence of Almighty

God who is also your Heavenly Father. Place yourself in the embrace of his love and let your eyes roam around your chosen picture until your attention is caught in some way. Linger with that aspect, as you enter more fully into what has been awakened in you. Let the picture and all that it represents speak into your situation, as you pray around whatever theme or themes emerge.

You may find it helpful to return to this theme in your next prayer time, and to go on using that picture for as long as it speaks to you. Using the same picture on later occasions may also take you further into the process.

3. Make a collage of your life as it seems to you at the moment. Stick together pictures from a magazine, or coloured shapes that appeal to you. If you consider that your life is in a tangle, then add some knotted string, or coloured threads. Small shells, pasta shapes, rice grains, leaves, twisted sweet wrappers . . . there is no end to the common objects you can use. Contemplate your production, see what it says about your attitudes, thoughts and feelings, and turn them into prayer.

TO HELP YOU GET GOING
Read the small book *Let Your Artist Out* by William Derring (New Alresford: Hunt and Thorp, 1992).

8

Writing as Prayer

Remember all the way which the
LORD your God has led you.
(Deuteronomy 8:2 RSV)

It is comforting to realise that you do not have to have an A in English to use writing as part of your prayer. Since you are writing for your eyes alone you do not need to worry about spelling (always a problem for me), punctuation or grammer. Writing for this purpose is a means to an end, not the end itself. It is thinking your thoughts through the point of your pen, in the presence of God; a way of opening yourself to him.

Many people find it helpful to write out quotations, prayers, Bible passages and hymns that are especially meaningful to them. Some like to paste in pictures that illustrate the theme, and others make their own illustrations in a variety of ways. In this manner the words are enhanced by there being a more visual impact. Yet others like to write out the words, indeed every letter, slowly and in their best, most careful writing or in capital letters, as they meditate on the meaning and application of the selected passage. The pictures, the lettering and the whole layout together make something that is pleasing and beautiful, honouring to the God of beauty and creativity.

Another use of writing as prayer is to take a passage of Scripture and make a paraphrase, expressing its essential meaning in your own words. When you use contemporary idiom you can bring out the force and application of the passage, and turn it into your own prayer. Once when I was helping with a workshop entitled something like More Ways Into Prayer we asked the participants to write a prayer about some everyday activity. Doing this in prose, poetry or the style of a psalm is actually easier than many people believe. A number on this workshop said they could not possibly do it, but we deliberately offered no alternative for that session, and in the end people found the exercise very helpful. From those who were willing to share what they had produced we had, amongst others, prayers based on entering the office, letter writing, taking a shower, doing the ironing, the washing-up suds, the computer, silk painting, embroidery and following retirement.

Here is an example from that very workshop. It was written by someone who had not attempted poetry before, but who has since been encouraged to repeat the practice.

The Computer

Switch on
Load the memory

Give the command
Create –
    format
    font
    enter

Oh God, Darn it, ERROR

Repeat

    EXIT, PRINT, STORE – GOOD GOD

Lord, switch me on to your power

Remind me yet again
of your call and command
to create in me what you will
Set within your frame and format
Enter every word and process
Forgive the error of my ways
Repeat your word for my condition
Restore in me your perfect will

Father, Son and Holy Spirit.

There is nothing, absolutely nothing, that cannot become the seed thought to spark off a heart-felt prayer. Seeing an old and familiar truth in contemporary living conditions, and praying it through in the medium of writing, is always an interesting and rewarding undertaking. In his book *Prayers of Life*[1] Michel Quoist includes prayers on such diverse subjects as a Five Pound Note, The Pornographic Magazine, The Tractor, Hunger,

Housing, The Bald Head, Posters and many others. There are numerous such collections available, it is worth looking at some in your local library or Christian bookshop.

At times it may be helpful to move from the particular to the general, shifting from the close-up to the panoramic view. Often this can be done most revealingly in the form of a story, either a fairy story or one about some aspect or epoch in your own life, or perhaps about things that you would like to have done differently. At other times an historical approach may be called for, writing a personal history or your faith story.

It might sometimes be helpful to write letters – letters that are not meant to be sent, but which are written as a means of sorting out conflicting feelings and attitudes. Sometimes this device of unsent letters is a useful way of articulating to ourselves things that need to be said but which, for whatever reason, are not possible to say at the time. In the presence of God, and the knowledge of his forgiveness and unconditional acceptance, wrongs can be confessed, and painful goodbyes said. When written to someone who has died it is not the same as contacting or communicating with the dead, but is a way of completing one's own unfinished business. It is undertaken in order to let go of the past, shake off the fetters that continue to bind, and become free to move on again.

For some people, at some time in their lives, the most meaningful prayers flow from the end of their pens. But perhaps 'flow' is the wrong word, for unfinished sentences and ungrammatical phrases are often mixed with random, seemingly disconnected thoughts that push their way into the mind and onto the page as the prayer is forming. In times of uncertainty or confusion, at any time of groping after the clarification that remains just beyond reach, writing about what is going on within oneself frequently moves the process on a few steps. Writing out thoughts, feelings and reactions, the whole gamut of wanderings and wonderings within, is like turning the focusing wheel on a pair of binoculars. A glazed, hazy blur gradually resolves, until suddenly everything is in clearer focus.

In times of difficulty or indecision we often need the clarity that comes when what is going on within can be externalised. 'Talking it through' is a time-honoured way to do this, but sometimes more privacy is required, or there just isn't anyone available. There are a variety of ways in which writing can provide this way of externalising, and so making some sort of sense of, the jumble within. Many people are helped by writing out their reflections on the day, or following some particular period in their lives, or during any time of uncertainty, difficulty or perplexity. Some people I know are very methodical and like to do this almost every day. Others are more random in their lifestyles and prefer to do so episodically, when there is some particular need, or they just have the urge to write again.

the presence of the Lord

was not in the wind
that shattered the rocks

nor in the earthquake
that followed the wind

nor in the fire
that followed the earthquake

but in the gentle whisper
that followed the fire

Some write on whatever is handy at the time, others like to use a particular type of notebook, be it one with a beautifully bound stiff cover or an ordinary exercise book. It does not matter what you use, or how often, or when. Writing is one more fruitful way of praying for you to try.

I have kept an Occasional Journal for many years and find that unlined sheets in an attractive A4 ringbinder suits my somewhat nomadic lifestyle best. I only take the current sheet(s) with me when I travel, along with any other papers required for that trip, and periodically transfer used ones to their own file on my return home. Sometimes there are long gaps between entries, at other times I write more frequently and fluently. Sometimes it is a record of my thoughts on a Bible passage or a book that I am reading. At other times an entry will start off as a string of questions much as the psalmist did, and after a while an answer suggests itself. I may then question that, in a sort of dialogue, and 'think around' the subject through further writing.

There may be some resolution or answer there and then, or I may need to return to the matter at subsequent prayer times. Returning to the same subject several times is not the same as using vain repetition, nor does it mean that one is stuck in a rut. Rather it is a deepening and further processing of the subject matter so that it becomes digestable and usable, rather in the manner of a ruminant chewing the cud. Only when the flavour has gone and the cud finally swallowed, is it profitable to move on to another mouthful of grass, another subject for prayer.

Often I reflect within the privacy of my journal on a situation that I wish I had handled differently – truly Professor Mistake is the best of teachers! Frequently this is some reaction, or lack of action, on my part that does not do justice to an opportunity. Usually the root seems to come from the persistence of early childhood responses that need recognising and bringing into the healing light of Christ.

Here is one example, written when I was attending a short course to learn a new skill I had long been wanting to acquire. I realised that an old and all too familiar anxiety had reappeared and, as a consequence, I did not make as much use of the time as I had expected and wanted. This is an extract from the relevant entry in my journal.

> I am aware of my inner child, an anxious child – told to wait for the teacher, wanting to get on, yet fearful of 'getting it wrong' if I proceed before she gets round to me and instructs me properly. *In this way I stifle my initiative, do not trust my intuition, and **paralyse myself**.*

I was recognising a pattern running through my life at the time. The entry continues:

> Also I lose the greatest lesson, from making

mistakes!

I do not have to 'get it right', only to have a go.

I do not have to 'wait for teacher', only to wait on God.

What happens if I get it wrong? Frowning disapproval.

Parental disapproval = God's disapproval. Withdrawal of love

and acceptance = God's disappearance.

My equation – if I get it wrong, God will disappear;

my security, my foundation will shatter.

THAT'S A LIE.

Replace it with: 'If I get it wrong GOD WILL APPEAR to HELP.

God chose foolish – weak – lowly – despised things and people, and such am I.

I STAND FIRM IN THE GOD WHO COMES IN LOVE.

So writing is one way of getting things in perspective, of beginning to see them from God's point of view. Setting the situation down on paper, considering it and praying it through seems to be one way that we can work with God to bring about some needed changes. It is one way in which old wounds can begin to be healed. Areas that have become stunted through fear, anxiety, mistrust and other maladaptive responses adopted early in childhood, can be released. Habits that have been acquired, however long ago they were learnt, can be replaced with more appropriate practices.

Writing down reflections in times of struggle and puzzlement sometimes seems to be a hard and pointless task, but it is frequently the opening of a window onto the situation. It reminds me of an incident that occurred when I was on holiday some years ago. Toiling up the long route of Snowdon with two friends we happened to overhear the conversation of a group who were on their way down. It almost put us off continuing with our climb. Apparently there was so much cloud and mist around at the top that they had seen nothing of the fabled view, although they had stopped as long as they could. One said he had been up seven times and still had never seen the view! We decided to press on and sure enough at the summit we found ourselves just above a thick blanket of clouds.

We hung around a bit, feeling quite disconsolate. As we continued to look we were amazed to see the clouds parting. The gap grew, the sun shone, and soon we were looking at an astounding sunlit panorama far below. We were indeed fortunate, for all too soon, more clouds rolled in and that stunning bird's- eye view was once more hidden from us. On the descent we were able to savour the magnificent vista that we had been privileged to see from the summit. Somehow the slow parting of the clouds had made the unfolding revelation of the scene below even more breathtaking, it was more special than if we had seen it all at once, as soon as we had arrived. The clouds were themselves part of the experience.

Writing is one way of coping with the clouds, and finding a way through the fog. Continue to write and reflect and a gap will open up, the sun will emerge and throw its light on the scene. When clouds come and go in the different seasons of life, taking up a pen and writing about the issues under the cloud, while inviting the Son of Man to shed his own light on the scene, does bring some clarity and illumination to the subject.

In more routine times I find that it is a useful and economical habit to jot down any key phrase that reverberates for me after any time of reading and prayer. The very act of recalling it to mind and writing it down helps to fix the phrase in my memory, and I find that it will then slip in and out of my awareness at intervals during the day. This enables me to meditate on it while engaged in many customary activities that do not take much thinking about. For most of us there are many short (hopefully!) times of waiting around for something to happen; the traffic lights to change in our favour, in a queue, for a train or bus, for a meeting to start, the kettle to boil, a phone call to come in. All of us have many little waiting times that we can utilise with profit.

During this process of turning such thoughts over in the mind throughout the day, other aspects of the subject are likely to come to mind, shedding new light on the issues. Frequently the whole topic tends to expand during the day as new aspects are linked up with fresh thoughts pulled out from the memory store. It is often fruitful to record these expansions on the theme at the next time of prayer, and to carry on from there. In this way prayer and daily life are not two separate activities, but become woven into one another as a seamless garment.

Calligraphy is another form of writing that particularly lends itself to prayer. The whole act of writing, the choosing of the pen and the writing surface used, as well as the words portrayed and any illustrative embellishments, are all part of the discipline and the art. The word calligraphy is derived from two Greek words, *kalli* meaning beauty and *graphia* to write. So calligraphy has to do with both the enjoyment and the beauty of the act of writing itself, and with the interpretation of what is being written. It is concerned with the very process of writing as well as with the product.

I well remember a colleague who was learning to write in the classical Chinese way. He would sit down in a quiet, composed way and slowly, methodically grind his own ink from an inkstone. He did this with great deliberation), for he had been instructed that the very thoughts he entertained while doing so would influence the way he formed the characters he would be writing. He knew that it was essential to have a time of composure before commencing to write, and to remain reflective during the whole time that he was writing.

Calligraphy lends itself to the development of such an attitude, and when used as prayer it certainly requires that disposition. It is important to let go of all other preoccupations, however legitimate they are, and to concentrate solely on the present moment, on this one venture. The whole business of choosing the colours to be used, of taking care in forming the letters well and then placing the words and the phrases so that the entire layout makes a pleasing impact – becomes a part of worship. When concentrating on the meaning of the words the writing becomes the prayer, and the prayer occurs with the writing.

When I was learning my first script I soon realised that I had to keep my eyes on the original copy, and follow only that. There was a very strong temptation to copy the line immediately above, which was the one that I had just done. When I did this then all I was doing was copying my own mistakes all the time. I had to keep reminding myself to return to the original teaching material, not my version of it; a salutary reminder to keep my eyes on Christ, not on my own activities.

SOME BOOKS TO HELP YOU

Life Path, Luci Shaw (Crowborough: Christina Press, 1997).

Paper Pilgrimage, Lawrence Osborn (London: Daybreak, 1990).

Keeping a Spiritual Journal, Edward England (Godalming: Highland Books, 1988).

Be Creative

1. Think of the thing you most like doing. Write a poem of praise to God about it.
   Think of the least liked aspect of your life and turn your thoughts and feelings, your questions and aspirations about it into a prayer. Be honest with yourself, and with God.

2. Write your life story. You could look at it in 'houses I have lived in'; 'people who influenced me'; or the stages such as pre-school, school, teenage years, employment, and so on. Note your relationship with God, and with key people, throughout.

3. Choose an incident currently in the national or local news about which you are concerned.
   Write three letters regarding it – one to your MP, one to a friend and one to God.
   Then write three replies, one from each of them. What do the similarities and differences between these letters tell you about your current relationship with God? Talk to him about this.

9

Praying with Clay

'Like clay in the hand of the potter,
so are you in my hand.'
(Jeremiah 18:6)

I stood in the potter's square in a town in Nepal and watched fascinated, as the shapeless lumps of clay in the middle of the wheels rose up, as if alive, under the potter's hands, to become a storage jar for water, a flat dish for holding curds or a cooking pot. They made it seem so easy, but I knew it was a skill developed over many years and passed on from father to son. The clay is black when it is dug up out of the ground, but becomes a rich terracotta when baked in the Nepali's wood-fired kilns. Would I ever be able to do anything like that?

Standing in the sunshine with the snowcapped mountains in the distance painted glistening white against the deep blue sky, I thanked God for all the experiences he had brought me through. Some had been pleasant and some 'fiery', but all had come through his loving hands for the shaping of my life. Remembering again the story of the Potter's House in Jeremiah chapter 18, I prayed that the Lord would go on moulding my life. My interest in clay was born, and I now also use it in my prayer life.

My first term in India as a missionary doctor had been a marvellous experience in many ways. I had come to love the village people who made up most of our patients, but there had also been some very traumatic experiences, and I felt emotionally scarred. Then at home I was involved in a car accident and sustained a severe head injury, so I was physically scarred as well. In answer to many people's prayers I made a remarkable recovery from that, so I knew God's hand was on my life, but I still felt emotionally scarred. The Lord knew that too and drew my attention to the Jeremiah passage where the potter was making a pot on the wheel, but the pot he was shaping from the clay was marred in his hands (v 3). But he did not discard it as being of no use, he formed it into another pot, shaping it as seemed best to him. Then he says,

'Can I not do with you as this potter does?' (v 4).

That question went straight to my heart, and I knew he was saying to me: 'Those things which you think of as scars are really part of the pattern I am making of your life.' That was a tremendously healing experience for me and I felt restored and recommissioned for the next stage of my service. I wonder if you have scars in your life that you would like God to heal and use in his pattern for your life?

Afterwards there followed eighteen years in Nepal, years full of hard work, challenge, tears, laughter and above all joy in seeing God's hand at work in healing bodies and souls. When I finally came home to stay, I was eager to learn more about pottery, and started going to classes and eventually obtained my own wheel and kiln. Of course it is not necessary to have a wheel in order to make things out of clay. Many things can be made by what is called hand building. The clay can be moulded into any shape the maker has in mind, sometimes using coils or slabs. Even without knowing anything about pottery, it can sometimes be helpful to pray with a lump of clay in the hands, moulding it as we are prompted. It may speak back to us in a way that is significant.

Many people I have known, without any experience at all, have made objects which have meant a great deal to them at that stage in their lives. One young woman, who was about to get married, made a flat dish that was completely empty, signifying her openness to whatever the future held. In one

way she found that scary, but she trusted the Lord. Another person found himself making a small figure with what looked like bars all around. This made him realise that there were things in his life which were hindering him. One friend, while meditating on the story of Jesus washing the disciples' feet, made a chair. She already had a little figure that fitted, so she put that in, and made a basin for its feet. For several days afterwards whenever she caught sight of it she was reminded of the application of this story.

I once made the shape of a cormarant sitting on a post, drying its wings. It was shortly after I had retired and I felt as if I were drying my wings ready for another take off. One simple thing to do involves flattening a piece of clay or dough and cutting round a hand placed flat on it. Then a small object can be placed in it, to indicate something you want to offer to the Lord, or to receive from him. One person used her pottery hand as a candle-holder that constantly reminded her of how she, herself, was being held by God.

The more I learn about the pottery process the more it becomes clear that every stage has its significance for our spiritual and daily lives. Several times in the Bible God is described as the potter and we the clay. For example, Isaiah says in chapter 64 verse 8: 'O LORD you are our Father. We are the clay, you are the potter; we are all the work of your hand'. So making things with clay can become part of devotional life. Prayer is not just asking but an on-going communication with God.

Look with me at the pottery process, step by step, and perhaps you will see some significance for your life. I hope, too, that you will try making things out of clay, and begin to pray with clay. Clay sitting in the bin is not much good to anybody. Once it is in the potter's hands, he can make anything he has a mind to. In the same way, if we allow our heavenly Potter to take us into his hands, the potential is enormous.

There are many kinds of clay; earthenware, stoneware, porcelain, and many variations, different colours, different constituents. We have to work WITH the clay, not against it, getting to know it, its characteristics and capabilities. We cannot force it to behave in a way that it is not capable of. In the same way, I believe, God works with us. He made us, he knows us, understands our particular personalities and peculiarities, and will not force us to become someone who is just not us. However, he is such a skilful potter, that we may be surprised to discover what he can do with us if we give him the chance!

First comes the preparation of the clay, which takes longer than actually forming the pot on the wheel, and musn't be skimped. God doesn't hurry over preparing us for whatever he has in mind either. The clay has to be thoroughly mixed with the hands, so that there are no hard bits that would later spoil the shape, and so it is completely malleable. Are there hard bits in our personality, that the Lord wants to soften so that he can mould us? Next the clay has to be lifted up and thrown down hard on the table many times in different planes, to force out any air bubbles which may cause a weak spot. If any are left when it comes to firing in the kiln, they will explode and maybe shatter nearby pots too. We often have weak spots in our character, which show up at critical times and sadly we sometimes hurt other people. Looking back over my life, that has sometimes been true of me, and I have to ask the Lord's forgiveness. Our Potter works with us to get rid of those too, even when we feel pressurised from all sides.

The centring of the clay in the middle of the wheel is probably the most important part of the whole process. With the wheel spinning fast, the two hands gradually bring the clay into the centre. If this is not done accurately the pot will become lopsided, and may even spin off the wheel. Once it is properly centred the rest is comparatively straightforward. How true this is of our lives! If we do not keep centred on the Lord Jesus, things tend to go wrong. There was a time when I got off centre and began to take a direction that was not God's will for me. When I finally realised what was happening, and backtracked, it was a great relief to find that my life once more became balanced and harmonious.

All this time, the clay must be kept wet, otherwise it will become dry and brittle. It must remain malleable in the potter's hands. We all go through times of spiritual dryness; even the greatest of saints confess to such experiences. One time in Nepal, when I had been working extremely hard doing medical work, and we were not seeing much in the way of spiritual results, I began to wonder if it was all worth it. While trekking to a medical out-post and crossing the dry bed of a river, I sat on a rock in the middle. Looking around me, it seemed that my spirit was just like what I saw, grey and dry. The only affirmation of faith I could muster was 'My heart is fixed, trusting in the Lord'. However the Lord was gracious and shortly afterwards we experienced an outpouring of his Spirit. We do so need the Living Water to keep us fresh and responsive to his loving hands.

Sometimes something does go wrong and the pot

is marred in the potter's hands. Perhaps there was a weak spot in the clay, or perhaps it was just tired. If the clay is worked too much it may get tired and collapse. If that happens it is no good going on until it has had a rest. Then you can use it again. That is so true to life! We are only human, and we do get tired. When that happens, our understanding Heavenly Father does not scold us. He says 'Take a rest'. As he says in Matthew chapter 11 verse 28, 'Come to me, all you who are weary and burdened, and I will give you rest'. Then, when we are rested and restored, like the clay we can start again. Once more the clay must be centred, hollowed out, and the sides gently pulled up.

When I was doing this for the first time I remember my teacher saying, 'Pretend you are climbing inside the bowl and working from the inside out'. That seemed to be such a significant picture of the Holy Spirit working within us to produce his fruit. Depending on the shape required, the pot may be opened up at this stage to form a wider dish. We, too, may need opening up as Christians. For some reason, perhaps because we have been hurt earlier in life, we become closed in on ourselves and are frightened to let go. Then, gently, the Lord shows us that it is safe to open up to him and to others and let his light and love pour in. It feels risky, but is well worth it! When I was young I was very shy and scared of showing people the real me. It took years and a liberating work of the Holy Spirit to take away that fear.

Once the pot is the shape and size the potter wants, it has to be cut off the wheel and put on a shelf to dry. Cutting-off experiences are part of life, and they may not be pleasant at the time. Changes of job, moving house, retiring or losing someone near to us are forms of bereavement that we have to cope with. Coming home from Nepal to stay was an enormously stressful experience. My mother had died and there was a change of country, climate, language, culture and most of all, role. It took about three years before I began to feel normal again, although I had a job in General Practice. In a way it was a drying-off experience, a necessary time of adjustment, just as it is necessary for the pot to dry off before it is handled again.

Have you ever felt you are 'on the shelf'? I am not just thinking of being unmarried, but rather of times in our lives when for some reason we are inactive and we may feel useless. It may be because of ill health or some other limitation, but just as it is an important stage for the pot, so it is for us. It is something that has to happen to prepare us for the next part of the process and of our journey. So we can be at peace and trust the Lord in this too.

When the clay is leather hard it is turned upside down on the wheel to finish off the base. Have you felt turned upside down by events? I certainly have; it is not a pleasant sensation, but that too is often used by the Lord to make us more stable Christians. At this point the potter may decide to engrave a design on the outside of the pot. This reminds me of the scars I thought were made on me, but which turned out to be part of God's pattern. You may have hurts which have remained with you; trust the Lord to turn them into assets. The last thing the potter does before firing, is to inscribe his name or insignia on the base of the pot, and that is what God does for us. He stamps his own name on us for ever.

When they are completely dry, but still very fragile, the pots are stacked in the kiln for the first firing. This applies to hand-built models as well as those made on the wheel. The kiln is heated up to a very high temperature, then allowed to cool enough to open. On opening up one of the first things you notice is that the clay has changed colour. Like the Kathmandu clay it may have been black to start with, but is now a rich terracotta. Also as you handle the pots you realise they are much stronger. Of course, if you dropped them on a concrete floor they would break, but they are strong enough for ordinary use. We all go through fiery experiences at times in our lives, which are very difficult while they last. Certainly they change us, and in time we will realise that they have strengthened us in ways that nothing else could.

So now we have a collection of pots and models that have been through the firing process, but that doesn't usually mean they are ready for use, unless they are flower pots. If you put water in them now, they would leak. They need to be glazed and fired again. This not only makes them waterproof, but more decorative as well. This is an exciting part of the process. Glazes are of many sorts and colours, and can be dipped, sprayed, poured or brushed on. But there is often an element of unpredictability about it. The colours change according to the temperature and length of firing, as well as other factors. It is always exciting to open the kiln after a glaze firing. I'm glad that our lives are not always predictable, it would be so boring if they were! But on the other hand I'm glad that our Heavenly Father is never taken by surprise. He knows what is round the corner for us, and makes sure it all works for our good.

After the glaze firing, we put them all out on the table. They are all shapes and sizes and all have different uses, just as we are all different, with differing characteristics and gifts. But unlike these pots, which to all intents and purposes are finished, God is never finished with us until we meet him face to face.

I wonder what God wants to do with you at this stage?

Suggestions for Prayer Activity

1. Hold a lump of plasticine, playdough or soft clay in your hands, close your eyes and remember that you are the clay in your Heavenly Potter's hands. Feel it, mould it, change its shape without thinking much about it. After a few minutes,

open your eyes and look at it. Does it begin to look like something? If it does, work on it to make it more like that thing. For instance it may begin to look like a boat, or a shell, or an animal, bird or fish. Does this say anything about how you are at this moment? Is God saying anything to you through this? Turn it into prayer.

2. Choose a Bible story that appeals to you, and meditate on it, imaginatively. Then make something used or indicated in the story. It doesn't matter how simple or rudimentary it is. The purpose is not to create a masterpiece, but to listen and respond to God. Having made the object, ask God what significance it has for you, and turn that into prayer.

3. Make an object which represents something you would like to offer to God, or that you would like God to do for you or somebody else.

4. Make a simple plaque (flat plate) and inscribe on it some word or text that God seems to be saying to you. You can do this with a pencil, and make a design round it if you wish.

5. Consider the pottery process again, with its different stages and use prayerfully. You may be able to go to a pottery and watch the potter at work, or join an adult education class. Does any

of it 'ring bells' with your experience? Allow the Holy Spirit to minister to you and turn it into prayer.

Irenaeus, a second-century Bishop wrote:

Offer your heart to God in a soft and tractable state, that you may receive the impress of His fingers, lest being hardened you should escape His workmanship in your life.

10

Living Creatively

We know that all that happens to us is
working for our good if we love God
and are fitting into his plans.
(Romans 8:28 Living Bible)

'All that happens to us' is the material God uses to create something really good out of our lives. We can either co-operate with him, or not. That 'all' includes our personality, the family situation into which we are born, our gifts and abilities, weaknesses and quirks, the delights and the seeming tragedies that occur. Some of the stuff of our daily lives is totally out of our control, much is not. God wants to use everything for our ultimate benefit, but he needs our co-operation. So much depends on whether we have a creative, passive or negative attitude to life.

To live creatively we must practise seeing opportunities instead of problems, translating 'difficulty' as 'challenge'. It will make demands on us and stretch our ingenuity, but the result will be worthwhile. We may be very dissatisfied with what we make of our lives, but God is pleased with creative struggle and will often surprise us by using our efforts. Life is not so much about expertise, as trying to be creative in different ways, including in our prayer life. Creative living is an attitude of mind and heart.

A Nepalese boy was about thirteen when he was dragged into a mill by his clothes. His left arm was pulled off at the shoulder and both his legs were crushed. He was carried, more than half dead to our hospital, received several pints of missionaries' blood, but still nearly died on the operating table. We had to amputate both his legs, and it was a miracle that he lived. His family abandoned him, because they said he would be no good in the fields. So the hospital had to pay for all his treatment and food. Eventually, he made a good recovery and we were able to make him two wooden legs in our workshop. This very brave and determined young man would have to use his brain rather than his legs if he were to have any future.

We were able to contact his family in the village and explain to them that he was not useless; if he went to school, he would later be able to get a job and earn money. They didn't seem very convinced, but we sent him home with the assurance of our prayers. By then he had a simple faith. Many years later, when I was making a return visit, I asked after him, a message was sent to his village, and he came walking up to see me. By that time he had had a better pair of legs made for him in South India. Imagine my delight when he told me that he had passed his school exams, received some higher education, and was now Headmaster of the school, respected by the whole village. He had used his disability creatively and become the person he was capable of being.

An elderly friend of mine has been dreadfully crippled for many years. Life for her is a constant struggle, but she never speaks of her problems. When I visit her, I always come away cheered and inspired. Joni Earieckson Tada is one who, although paralysed from the neck down, has blessed many through her testimony and books. Etty Hillesum was a Dutch Jew, who kept a wartime journal from 1941 until she died in Auschwitz in 1943, aged twenty-eight. In the most appalling circumstances she gradually discovered her personal calling to live creatively in that situation. She wrote 'There is no hidden poet in me, just a little piece of God that might grow into poetry. And a camp needs a poet, one who experiences life there, even there, as a bard and is able to sing about it.'[1]

Most of the people around her didn't want to think, as it made them too depressed, but she prays: 'Let me be the thinking heart of these barracks.' Then she says, 'I have stopped making plans and worrying about risks. Happen what may, it is bound to be for the good.' In her short life, she was an inspiration to the whole camp. Whatever circumstances come our way, we can use them destructively or creatively.

Most of us do not have such enormous challenges

to face, but we all have difficulties of one kind or another. A single Mum does her best to bring up her children well, a widow runs a club for other widows, a blind or handicapped person who lives alone is determined not to be dependent on others. We also need to be creative in good and happy circumstances. If God has blessed us with sound health and a comfortable home we have a wonderful opportunity to use those things in an imaginative way, to give pleasure to others as well as ourselves.

We may have been given gifts or abilities that have remained undeveloped for various reasons, and then reach a stage in life when it is possible to activate one or two of those latent skills. Jesus tells us not to bury our talents in the ground, but develop them for our own and other people's pleasure or benefit. So find out what you would really love to do. Don't ignore the urge, it might be a nudge from God. This means not only artistic talent, but things like DIY, perhaps, or hospitality, you may have an affinity for animals, the ability to relate to children or elderly people, and there are many more forms of voluntary work. For instance, car drivers are needed by many organisations such as 'Meals on Wheels' and the Hospital Car Service. Even a good sense of humour can be used by God! 'For we are God's workmanship [some translations say poem], created in Christ Jesus to do good works, which God prepared in advance for us to do' (Eph 2:10).

We have been looking at people who have managed to have a positive outlook in spite of great difficulties, but I am not advocating an unrealistic kind of hearty optimism in all circumstances. That could be unkind and unhelpful. If someone we know has suffered a great loss or tragedy, we need to listen and try to empathise with their feelings. If we ourselves experience something devastating, it is normal to feel dreadful and we should allow ourselves to grieve. It doesn't help to repress our feelings, which should be expressed in some way.

It has been said that 'Impression without expression leads to depression'. Weeping is often therapeutic. At that stage to say 'Cheer up it will all turn out all right in the end' is intensely irritating, but I am making a plea for us to accept everything that comes our way in life, welcome or unwelcome, as an opportunity for creative thinking and openness to God. If we want to live a full, enjoyable and productive life, so much depends on our attitude to our circumstances, and attitude is often a matter of choice.

Many people in industrialised countries today find that their greatest challenge is to bring a creative attitude to their work. Some are so busy, so caught up in their duties, that they are totally absorbed when at their jobs, and generally exhausted much of the rest of their time. They have to find ways of preventing their work taking over the whole of their lives, their very selves. It takes great determination and creativity for them to make time for their families, for some social life and adequate recreation. A number do manage to develop a prayerful attitude that pervades all those areas of life.

Other people have long periods of tedium to contend with at work. For them the challenge is to find ways of remaining lively, interesting people, whilst doing routine and unstimulating jobs, instead of switching off until the end of their working day. Sadly some only get through the day by dreaming about their evening and weekend lives. The creative ones find ways of remaining alert to the present moment, by making sure that whatever they do, they accomplish really well 'as unto the Lord'.

They find some aspect of their job, or their hours spent there, to be proud of; their tidiness, their punctuality, speed, accuracy or general helpfulness. There are people doing repetitive work that doesn't need concentration who find in it an opportunity for prayer.

Living creatively is about finding more satisfying ways of being a person. It is concerned with the struggle and pleasure of becoming the human BEING that accords with the particular design of the Creator God. For much of life we are caught up with so much busyness that we rob ourselves of the joy of simply being. Many are so engrossed doing the important things that 'have to' be done that they have little time for that which is necessary and life-sustaining. They have found no room for the truly fulfilling things in life, and so their lives remain unfulfilled.

Creative people have learned to use the right side of their brains as well as the left. They look at situations from a variety of angles and from unusual viewpoints, seeking alternative solutions. They are inclined to 'walk around' trouble spots, viewing them from inside and outside until a possible way forward is found. They are likely to ask themselves 'what else might be done', keeping an open mind regarding options. They realise there is always another viewpoint, as in the old adage, 'two men looked out from prison bars: one saw mud the other stars'. The more recent high street version of this is one person moaning about his cup being half empty, while another rejoices that his is half full. It all depends on where our attention is focused.

Relationships make up most of our lives in one way or another. Good ones need working at, they don't just happen, although the initial contact may. In marriage, friendship, at work and with neighbours, we must face rather than avoid difficulties and conflicts. If we try to find ways of meeting each other in non-threatening situations, then we might begin to see another side to the person with whom we tend to clash. Hopefully this will enable us to talk about and respect our different approaches to life, and to laugh together about those issues which would otherwise remain as serious irritants.

The natural instinct to defend ourselves and retaliate when someone hurts us is the stuff out of which wars are made, but God has called us to love our enemies. Morris Stuart makes the point very clearly, 'Love of our enemy is a creative action which interrupts the cycle of evil justifying evil, hurt justifying retaliation. Far from being a soft option, a pious response or simply submission to that which is evil, love of our enemy is a creative response which has the possibility of turning the enemy into a friend.'[2] Love creates, it does not destroy.

The kind of body and mind we have is part of God's gifting to us, as is our personality, which Ruth has written about in her book *Personality and Prayer* in this series. We all have different personalities, which largely come to us in our genes, although they may be modified, to some extent, by training and circumstances. It is not a matter of 'right' or 'wrong' or 'good' or 'bad' or 'Christian' or 'unChristian', but merely of 'difference'. The more we understand our particular strengths, the better we will be able to live creatively to God's glory, and minimise our weaknesses. People who try to force themselves into someone else's mould will not make a very good job of it.

Engaging in any creative activity, whether it be painting, pottery, writing, embroidery, gardening, making a cake, running a home or anything else, tends to develop in people a positive attitude to life. This cannot be separated from our prayer life, as Christ's Spirit lives within us. When God created the world and everything in it, he loved what he had made. When we create anything, whether it is knitting a sweater or building a relationship, if we do it with love, it is much more effective than doing it merely from a sense of duty. The Bible teaches us to love God and our neighbours as ourselves. It says 'as ourselves' not 'instead of ourselves' so it is important that we love the person that God has created, and co-operate with him in living our lives creatively.

We are not only 'human beings' but also 'human becomings'. This attitude is closely related to our sense of call, as Christians. God has created each one of us for a purpose, and he works in us and with us to fulfil that purpose. When we are fitting in to his plan, it is amazing what he can do with us.

We need to stop rushing through life and listen to what he has to say. Each one of us is called, not only missionaries and ministers. That calling may vary at different stages of our lives. For instance my role as a retired person is very different from when I was in full-time employment, but I am still the same person. I have slowed down somewhat and now have time to do things I could not fit in alongside my work.

It is necessary to reflect from time to time, and consider what is the most creative way of using our time and energy at any particular stage. Painting a picture or making a sculpture generally takes a long time. It doesn't do to hurry. We live in such an 'instant' world that it becomes habitual to expect quick results. God is not like that; he works with us very patiently and we need to be patient with ourselves too. It takes courage to be creative, we must be prepared to take risks and to make mistakes. When setting out to paint a picture, there is nothing so daunting as a blank canvas or sheet of paper. Having overcome that fear and made some marks, it becomes somewhat easier.

So with life, it takes courage to move on and do something different or to do the same things differently, more creatively. Remember that God takes responsibility for his workmanship, and he hasn't finished with us yet. Ann Lewin has written a poem which makes that point very beautifully. It appears in her book *Candles and Kingfishers*:

God's work of art.
That's me?
Then beauty must lie
In the eye of the
Beholder.

I feel more like
One of those statues
Michelangelo left
Half emerging
From the marble block;
Full of potential,
On the verge of life,
But prisoned still
By circumstances and
Fear

Yet part of me is free –
And you are still creating,
Bringing to life
The promise that is there.

Sometimes by
Hammer blows
Which jar my being,
Sometimes by
Tender strokes half felt
Which waken me to
Life.

Go on, Lord.
Love me into wholeness.

Set me free
To share with you
In your creative joy;
To laugh with you
At your delight
In me,
Your work of art.[3]

Perhaps you had not realised you are God's work of art and you are his co-artist!

Suggestions for Prayer Activity

1. Look for stories in the Bible, where people have acted creatively in a difficult situation, e.g. Joseph, in good and bad times, or Paul and Silas in prison. Pray for those you know, who are going through bad times.

2. Look back on your own life. Were there times when you tackled problems with a creative outlook? Praise God for that. Is there something facing you now, that you would not have chosen? Ask for God's guidance on how to act.

3. Make a list of your known strengths and assets. How are they being used at present? Ask the Lord if there is some better way of using them. Have you been persuaded to adopt some role for which you know you are not cut out? Perhaps it is time to have the courage to step down, and make room for other things.

4. Above all, listen to God and be aware of how he is using all your circumstances to continue creating the work of art, which is you. Ask God to help you to discern the creative way of reacting in every situation.

Notes

Chapter 1
1. Margaret Guenther, *Toward Holy Ground* (London: DLT, 1996).

Chapter 2
1. SU notes *Alive to God*, 1996.
2. Brother Ramon, source unknown.
3. Brother Ramon, source unknown.
4. Ulrich Schaffer, source unknown.

Chapter 3
1. Richard Foster, *Prayer: Finding the Heart's True Home* (London: Hodder & Stoughton, 1992).
2. From the Foreword to Eddie Askew, *Cross Purposes* (Brentwood: The Leprosy Mission International, 1995).

Chapter 5
1. Article in *Healing and Wholeness*, May/June 1996.
2. SU notes, *Alive to God*, March 1997.
3. Graham Kendrick, *Christian Music*.

Chapter 6
1. From the Foreword to Anne Long, *Praise Him in the Dance* (London: Hodder & Stoughton).
2. V. Balchin, source unknown.
3. Sue Sutherland, *With All that Is Within Me*.

Chapter 7
1. Henri Nouwen, *The Return of the Prodigal Son* (London: DLT, 1994).

Chapter 8
1. Michel Quoist, *Prayers of Life* (Dublin: Gill, 1963).

Chapter 10
1. *Etty: A Diary 1941–43*, quoted by Francis Dewar in *Invitations* (London: SPCK, 1996).
2. SU notes, *Alive to God*.
   Ann Lewin, *Candles and Kingfishers* (Foundery Press, '97).